THE KIRKYARD OF JOHN KNOX (Aberdeen)

Foreword

Nestling behind John Knox Church, and literally a stone's throw away from the noisy Mounthooly roundabout, John Knox Churchyard is just the place for a quiet walk. No stone is older than 1835, for it was then that the original church was built to cater for the increasing population in this part of the city, between the New Town and the Old. The present church dates from 1911. There are no grand memorials here, and no famous personages, but there is plenty of interest nevertheless. Craftsmen, seamen drowned in distant waters, emigrants to the Colonies, young men killed in the Great Wars - all these and many other ordinary folk are remembered here in this little haven of peace.

It gives me special pleasure to present this transcription. Firstly because 1985 sees the 150th anniversary of the Church. Secondly, because my mother's family - the Scorgies - have been associated with the Church for the whole of this century. My parents were married here, and here I was baptised and went to Sunday School. Hardly a day goes by without a glance over to the graveyard, for I live but 200 yds away on the road to Old Aberdeen.

My thanks go to my wife for her help in this transcription, and without whose gentle prodding I would have continually set the work aside.

The cover shows the Church c.1911 and with the original wall and garden leading to the graveyard. Sadly, half the garden was removed when the street was widened to make the approach road to the roundabout.

R. Leith.

(The Society wish to thank Mr & Mrs Leith for their work in this churchyard. and the Editor also says thank you, as do the Graveyard Gang.)

SECTION A.

1a No Stone.

---

1 Erected by JAMES FALCONER in memory of his son WILLIAM COUTTS d. 17 Nov. 1885 aged 6 mths; the above JAMES FALCONER d. Geelong, Australia 6 Feb. 1895 aged 40; his son JAMES d. Greenburn, Campfield 30 Jan. 1899 aged 15.

---

2 In loving memory of my wife ELIZABETH GARDEN d. 15 May 1945 aged 84; her husband GEORGE DAWSON d. 16 June 1954 aged 90; also my father and mother.

---

3 In loving memory of our dear son WILLIAM STRUTHERS d. 24 Aug. 1896 aged 5½; also WILLIAM KYNOCH d. July 1867; CATHERINE MILNE wife of above WILLIAM KYNOCH d. 10 May 1894 aged 62; MARY KYNOCH d. 31 Aug. 1868 aged 6½; ROBERT KYNOCH d. 31 Mar. 1868 aged 5 mths.

4-6 No Stones.

---

7 D M 1879.

---

8 Erected by GEORGE S. MacKAY in memory of his father ALEXANDER MacKAY d. 5 Nov. 1864 aged 60; and his two brothers, JOHN MacKAY d. 31 Oct. 1860 aged 18; DANIEL MacKAY d. 6 Feb. 1856 aged 4 yrs 8 mths; WILLIAM MacKAY d. Hull 30 Nov. 1872 aged 32; JANET SINCLAIR wife of ALEXANDER MacKAY d. 18 Aug. 1904 aged 93.

---

9 No Stone

---

10 Erected in memory of CHRISTINA MURRAY the beloved wife of WILLIAM GALL d. 16 Mar. 1902 aged 72; said WILLIAM GALL d. 17 June 1906 aged 77; their daus. ELIZA GALL beloved wife of GEORGE STRACHAN farmer, Auchindreich, Bervie d. 29 Jan. 1919 aged 53; dau. MARGARET ROBINS GALL beloved wife of JAMES ROBERTSON F.C.I.S., Cults d. 23 Nov. 1920 aged 61; said JAMES ROBERTSON d. 15 Aug. 1931 aged 76.

---

11 In memory of JAMES son of JAMES SCOTT d. 31 Mar. 1873 aged 9 weeks; his dau. JEANNIE d. 25 May 1907 aged 27; his wife ANN SMITH d. 12 Aug. 1902 aged 50; said JAMES SCOTT stonecutter d. 18 Oct. 1904 aged 58.

---

12 Erected by ALEXANDER NEILSON in memory of his daus.-in-law, JESSY STEWART d. 6 Sept. 1837 aged 20; ELSPIT STEWART d. 21 Jan. 1838 aged 18; WILLIAM STEWART d. 13 Oct. 1838 aged 10.

---

13 No Stone.

---

14 Erected by MARGARET DURNO in memory of her father ROBERT DURNO d. 3 Jan. 1895 aged 75; her mother MARGARET DINGWALL d. 3 Jan. 1893 aged 69; her uncle ALEXANDER DURNO aged 75; above MARGARET DURNO b.3 Nov.1861 - d. 1 Jan. 1933

A.15 No Stone

16 Wee JOHNIE and ALICK's grave.

17 No Stone.

18 Erected by JAMES RAE in memory of his family JAMES d. 6 Apr. 1857 aged 7; HENRY d. 28 Dec. 1857 aged 2; JOHN d. 30 Mar. 1860 aged 8; his wife MARGARET DAVIDSON d. 23 Aug. 1886 aged 59; said JAMES RAE late merchant, Ferryhill d. 24 Jan. 1902 aged 77; also his wife ELSPET MURRAY d. 24 Jan. 1931 aged 70.

19 In loving memory of C.H. D.F. J.C. J.F.

20 Erected by THOMAS ROSS in memory of his family viz. THOMAS d. 11 Jan. 1863 aged 7; ANN d. 19 Aug. 1868 aged 8 mths; WILLIAM d. at sea 6 Aug. 1880 aged 21, and is interred in Annfield Cemetery, Liverpool; ISABELLA d. 14 Oct. 1881 aged 18; his wife ISABELLA MURRAY or ROSS d. 3 Oct. 1908 aged 74; the above THOMAS ROSS d. 27 Jan. 1909 aged 74.

21 M.W. born 1816 - died 14 Dec. 1895.

22 No Stone.

23 In loving memory of ALAN TASTARD aged 4; also my dear wife ANN GROAT TASTARD d. 2 Dec. 1947 and JOSEPH TASTARD aged 61.

24 Erected by WILLIAM WEBSTER in loving memory of his wife MARY CRUICKSHANK d. 24 Mar. 1898 aged 77; above WILLIAM WEBSTER d. 12 May. 1898 aged 79; dau.-in-law JANE SMITH SKINNER d. 21 Mar. 1924 aged 69; granddau. CHRISTINA INGRAM WEBSTER d. 15 Oct. 1931 aged 35; WILLIAM WEBSTER husband of above JANE SKINNER d. 25 May 1939 aged 77.

25 J. McP. in memory of J.C. McPHERSON d. 6 days. 1893.

26 No Stone.

27 In memory of JAMES DUNCAN d. 19 Apr. 1855 aged 50; his wife MARY McROBBIE d. 20 Mar. 1870 aged 68; their children JANE d. 24 Feb. 1827 aged 3 mths; JOHN d. 29 July 1833 aged 15 mths; ELIZABETH d. 19 May 1840 aged 14 mths; CHRISTINA d. 13 July 1842 aged 10 mths; WILLIAM d. 17 July 1848 aged 14 yrs; their grandchildren GEORGE DUNCAN d. 19 Nov. 1852 aged 3; JANE McKINZIE d. 8 Apr. 1853 aged 2 weeks; ALEXANDER DUNCAN d. 25 Dec. 1863 aged 1 month; MARY DUNCAN d. 23 Dec. 1865 aged 2 yrs 9 mths; JANE MANN DUNCAN d. 27 Dec. 1865 aged 10 mths.

A. 27 Erected by GEORGE CHASSER in memory of his aunt SUSAN CHASSER d. 24 Nov. 1881 also of JANET GREIG WOOD wife of GEORGE CHASSER d. Greenock 19 Nov. 1889 and is interred there.

---

28 No Stone.

---

29 No Stone

30a In loving memory of our dear mother ISABELLA GARDEN d. 9 Jan. 1960 beloved wife of JAMES HEWITT.

---

30 Erected by JOHN ALEXANDER in loving memory of his wife JEANNIE ADAM d. 29 Apr. 1894 aged 30; their only child FLORENCE S. d. 5 Mar. 1893 aged 1; his brother ALEXANDER d. 8 Apr. 1869 aged 7; his father ALEXANDER ALEXANDER d. 4 Jan. 1916 aged 82; his mother HELLEN WILLIAMSON d. 28 Dec. 1910 aged 86; his son JOHN ALEXANDER and his nephew WILLIAM McLAREN both d. in infancy.

---

31 In loving memory of my wife JEMIMA SIMPSON d. 15 Dec. 1948 aged 70; our sons EDWARD & JOHN d. in infancy; above JAMES MASSON d. 15 May 1959 aged 89.

In loving memory of little EDDIE aged 17 months.

---

32 1866. Erected by GEORGE LOW in memory of his children ELIZABETH d. 25 Mar. 1864 aged 10 mths; MARGARET d. 20 June 1866 aged 3; BARBARA d. 10 May 1868 aged 11; MARY d. 3 Jan. 1870 aged 3.

---

33 J. LAMB 1868.

---

34 Erected by FANNY BLACK in memory of her husband JAMES MALCOLM d. 7 Nov. 1870 aged 64; above FANNY BLACK d. 30 May 1888 aged 75.

---

35 No Stone.

---

36 In memory of my dear husband ALEXANDER McTAVISH d. 16 Mar. 1907 aged 36.

---

37 No Stone

---

38 No Stone.

---

39 No Stone

---

40 In memory of AGNES PURVIS wife of THOMAS SMITH d. 17 Aug. 1902 aged 38; their dau. WILLIAMINA d. 16 Sept. 1901 aged 2 yrs 10 mths; his beloved 2nd wife GRACE MATHIESON d. 25 Sept. 1924 aged 59; above THOMAS SMITH d. 31 June 1932 aged 68.

A. 41 Erected by THOMAS & JAMES MILNE in loving memory of ELSPIT WOOD beloved wife of THOMAS MILNE d. 8 Aug. 1909 aged 73; also of their 3 children d. in infancy.

---

42 The burial ground of WILLIAM MATHIESON 1864. His wife ANN FERGUSON d. 2 May 1863 aged 48; their son ALEXANDER MATHIESON d. 17 Mar. 1895 aged 40; the above WILLIAM MATHIESON d. 20 Aug. 1895 aged 80.

---

43 No Stone

---

44 Erectedby WILLIAM DUNCAN in memory of his wife ELIZABETH DAVIDSON d. 22 Apr. 1873 aged 64; his son CHARLES d. 16 June 1865 aged 19; also WILLIAM DUNCAN late overseer d. 8 June 1878 aged 73.

---

45 No Stone.

---

46 In memory of MARGARET MASSIE dau. of WILLIAM MASSIE d. 10 Mar. 1864 aged $3\frac{1}{2}$; his son CHARLES MASSIE d. 2 Nelson Lane, on14th Feb. 1895 aged 26; son ALEXANDER BROWN MASSIE d.at 27 Constitution St,, 19 Dec. 1904 aged 27; son THOMAS MASSIE painter d. Collington Hospital, Edinburgh 21 Dec. 1906 aged 36; MARTHA SIM beloved wife of WILLIAM MASSIE/Gas Inspector d. at $27\frac{1}{2}$ Constitution St., Aberdeen 15 June 1907 aged 68; the above WILLIAM MASSIE d. 30 Dec. 1912 aged 73; also WILLIAM MASSIE d. 16 Aug. 1929 aged 66, eldest son of the above William Massie.

(Reverse) Erected by MARGARET MARSHALL in memory of her husband JOHN MASSIE d. 15 June 1870 aged 58; their son THOMAS MASSIE drowned at Dunbar 15 June 1869 aged 14; their son CHARLES d. 31 Aug. 1872 aged 20; above MARGARET MARSHALL d. at Scatterburn 23 Jan. 1900 aged 86.

---

47 No Stone.

---

48 In loving memory of MARY A. McBEATTIE b. 2 Sept. 1927 - d. 2 Oct. 1927.

---

49 Erected by his son-in-law in memory of ALEXANDER GREIG d. 28 Sept. 1890 aged 60; his three children d. in infancy; his father ALEXANDER GREIG d. 14 Feb. 1886 aged 90; also CHRISTIAN JAMIESON wife of above ALEXANDER GREIG d. 2 July 1919 aged 78.

---

50 Erected by WILLIAM SPARK in memory of his beloved mother JANE LEGG d. 28 Apr. 1877 aged 72; his brother-in-law WILLIAM FINDLAY d. 5 Mar. 1872 aged 38; his niece WILLIAMINA SPARK FINDLAY d. 7 July 1889 aged 20; ELIZABETH NAPIER or HADDEN mother of the said WILLIAM FINDLAY d. 24 Mar. 1882 aged 40;the above WILLIAM SPARK d. 13 Mar. 1902 aged 60; ELIZABETH LEIGHTON FINDLAY d. 17 July 1922.

W.S. Little JANE and LIZZIE.

A.51 No Stone

---

52 Erected by CHARLES MENZIES in memory of his father JOHN MENZIES d. 18 Jan. 1864 aged 58; his sister JANE d. 5 Sept. 1878 aged 20; his mother MARGARET BURNETT d. 27 Nov. 1909 aged 91; and of his family CHARLES MENZIES d. 24 Nov. 1892 aged 2 days; ALFRED MENZIES d. 3 Mar. 1887 aged 5 mths; MAGGIE G. MENZIES d. 12 May 1893 aged 2; CATHERINE G. MENZIES d. 6 Nov. 1899 aged 7 mths; also CATHERINE MENZIES d. 11 Feb. 1903 aged 2; WILLIAM MENZIES d. 23 Feb. 1903 aged 3.

---

53 No Stone.

---

54 Erected by P. MAITLAND in memory of his wife CHRISTINA R. SCOTT d. 27 Apr. 1887 aged 33; also CHRISTINA & DAVID; also his father GEORGE MAITLAND d. 27 Jan. 1896 aged 79; his mother JANE SUTHERLAND d. 5 Jan. 1908 aged 81; the above P. MAITLAND d. 19 Sept. 1919 aged 60; ANN VASS his wife; also PETER MAITLAND presumed dead July 1950 aged 63, son of the above P. MAITLAND.

---

55 In loving memory of JANE COOPER wife of JOHN CLARK ironmoulder d. 13 Sept. 1929 aged 69; their dau. JANET CAMERON d. 17 Feb. 1895 aged 10½; the above JOHN CLARK d. 13 Mar. 1946 aged 66.

---

56 No Stone.

---

57 Erected by ELSPET COOPER in memory of her husband ALEXANDER REID d. 7 Jan. 1872 aged 53; their son ALEXANDER d. 24 Feb. 1877 aged 14; above ELSPET COOPER d. 25 Dec. 1893 aged 66.

---

58 1867. The Burial place of WILLIAM COUTTS, Painter, Aberdeen in memory of his children JOHN S.K. d. 16 Sept. 1838 aged 5; HELLEN d. 16 Sept. 1840 aged 5; WILLIAM d. 1 Sept. 1847 aged 14 mths; JOHN d. 18 Oct. 1848 aged 6; his beloved wife ISABELLA MURISON d. 23 Oct. 1867 aged 56; dau. MAGGIE CRUICKSHANK wife of ALEXANDER BRAND Baker, Portobello d. 10 Jan. 1870 aged 28 & is interred there; his dau. ISABELLA wife of J. IRONSIDE d. in Edinburgh 11 Mar. 1880 & is interred there; the above WILLIAM COUTTS d. 15 Apr. 1881 aged 70; his dau. HELEN wife of GEORGE DAWSON d. at Sydney, N.S.W. 14 Oct. 1891 aged 42 and is interred there.

---

59 Erected by WILLIAM BROWN in memory of his sister ISABELLA d. 19 Dec. 1837 aged 55; also MARGARET M. SMITH d. 13 Apr. 1842 aged 3; FERGUSON SMITH drowned off the Kentish Coast 25 Dec. 1860 aged 20; FERGUSON SMITH Lumsden d. 12 June 1882 aged 14 mths; FERGUSON SMITH writer d. 28 Oct. 1887 aged 70; MARGARET COUTTS relict of FERGUSON SMITH d. 12 Feb. 1899 aged 83; WILLIAM SMITH d. 24 Aug. 1914 aged 63; ALEXANDER SMITH d. 26 Feb. 1916 aged 71.

Section B.

1 Erected by GEORGE STEVENSON in memory of his children MARY ANN d. 22 May 1861 aged 7 mths; ISABELLA W. d. 16 Dec. 1861 aged 7 yrs; MARGARET W. d. 12 Jan. 1862 aged 2 yrs 10 mths; AGNES d. 11 July 1866 aged 2; above GEORGE STEVENSON d. 24 June 1877 aged 55; also JEANNIE . . . d 3 Jan. 1897 aged 27; his wife JANE WEBSTER d. 25 May 1903 aged 74.

---

2 Erected by JEAN & CHRISTIAN PATERSON in memory of thier beloved father JOHN PATERSON d. 11 Apr. 1873 aged 80; their mother CLEMENTINA MICHIE d. 14 May 1859 aged 68; also JAMES WALLACE Seaman, husband of the above CHRISTIAN PATERSON lost at sea 24 Nov. 1864 aged 40; their daus. ISABELLA d. 14 Nov. 1864 aged 5; JAMIMA d. 22 Mar. 1866 aged 6; CHRISTIANA d. 6 July 1894 aged 41; the above CHRISTIAN PATERSON d. 18 May 1896 aged 70; also WILLIAM EWEN husband of RACHEL WALLACE d. 3 July 1900 aged 46; their eldest dau. JANE WALLACE d. 21 Dec. 1912 aged 62; also RACHEL wife of the above WILLIAM EWEN d. 4 Aug. 1923 aged 66.

---

3 Erected by JOHN PATERSON in memory of his spouse CLEMENTINA MICHIE d. 14 May 1859 aged 68; his dau. CLEMENTINA d. 2 Nov. 1827 age 1 yr 5 mths; ANN d. 20 Apr. 1834 aged 17; ISABELLA d. 17 Mar. 1844 aged 21; ALEXANDER d. 17 Jan. 1851 aged 27; the above JOHN PATERSON d. 11 Apr. 1873 aged 80; his son GEORGE PATERSON d. 31 Oct. 1880 aged 48.

---

4 No Stone.

---

5 Erected by JOHN THOM Joiner Aberdeen in memory of his son JOHN d. 17 Mar. 1880 aged 15; his dau. JANE d. 9 Jan. 1882 aged 20; MARGARET MORRISON his wife d. 13 Mar. 1882 aged 39; MARGARET SHEARER his mother-in-law d. 16 Mar. 1882 aged 65; FREDERICK his son d. 16 June 1882 aged 20 mths; JOHN GOODBRAND his son d. 28 Mar. 1885 aged 14 mths; MARJORY THOM d. 1 Oct. 1890 aged 3 yrs 9 mths; the said JOHN THOM d. 14 Mar. 1915 aged 74.

---

6 No Stone.

---

7 In memory of MAGGIE A.H. ANDERSON 1907 - 1929; also our dear children who died in infancy; their father ALEXANDER R. ANDERSON 1887 - 1961; their mother MAGGIE A. HALL 1886 - 1968; son-in-law NORMAN ROSS 1912 - 1977.

---

8 No Stone

---

9 No Stone

---

10 Erected by WILLIAM NEWELL in loving memory of his wife GEORGINA GORDON d. Aug. 1898.

---

11 No Stone

B.12 In loving memory of my dear wife LILY ANN ANDERSON d. 31 Oct. 1906 aged 21.

13 In loving memory of JAMES HAY d. 1912; his wife AGNES BAXTER d. 1881; their dau. CHRISTINA d. 1945.

14 In fond memory of PEGGY from P.R. Staff.

15 Erected by RICHARD DONALD & ANN GORDON his wife in memory of their 9 children d. in infancy; also ANNIE d. 10 Apr. 1873 aged 15; our grand children RICHARD D. McPHERSON d. 15 Mar. 1891 aged 6½; granddau. ANNIE SMITH d. 11 June 1899 aged 3; their youngest grandchild GEORGINA SMITH d. 10 Jan. 1914 aged 4 yrs 11 mths; the above ANN GORDON d. 13 Jan. 1914 aged 78; above RICHARD DONALD d. 11 Nov 1915 aged 87.

16 No Stone.

17 No Stone

18 In memory of ROBERT LING d. 21 Apr. 1846 aged 51; his son ARCHIBALD d. . . . dau. JANE d. 24 Oct. . .(stone broken)

19 In memory of JAMES HARPER d. 20 Jan. 1898.
Little JIM lies here.

20 Erected by WILLIAM DUNCAN engineer in loving memory of his sons ALEXANDER WILSON d. 5 Mar. 1897 aged 3 yrs 10 mths; Corporal EDWARD GORDON d. of wounds in France 7 Oct. 1918 aged 27; the above WILLIAM DUNCAN d. 1 June 1921 aged 81; his wife CATHERINE FORBES d. 11 June 1936 aged 77.

21 No Stone

22 Erected by JAMES REITH in memory of his wife MARGARET M. SHIRRAS d. 15 Dec. 1875 aged 37; his son J. ALEXANDER d. 14 1879 aged 22mths; JANE his dau. d. 23 Dec. 1879 aged 14; M.A. REITH or LAING his dau. d. 21 Nov. 1889 aged 24; ISABELLA DOW also wife of the above d. 31 May 1906 aged 73; the above JAMES REITH d. 27 Jan. 1916 aged 76; dau. AGNES H. d. 17 Sept. 1951 aged 78; JESSIE d. 5 Aug. 1955 aged 84. (Small stone) Little JAMI & JEANNIE'S grave 1879

23 No Stone

24 No Stone

25 In memory of WILLIAM WILSON d. 6 July 1861 aged 53; also MARY WILSON d. 9 Feb. 1856 aged 6; ALEXANDER WILSON d. 14 June 1870 aged 15; ANN MAIR wife of above WILLIAM WILSON d. 31 May 1904 aged 86; ANN WILSON d. 14 Jan. 1926 aged 77; MAY WILSON d. 12 Nov. 1936 aged 91.

B.26 Erected by ALEXANDER GREIG in memory of ISABELLA d. 14 July 1868 aged 2; WILLIAM d. 7 Jan. 1876 aged 3; VIOLETTA d. 15 July 1878 aged 8; BARBARA ANDERSON wife of the above ALEXANDER GREIG d. 25 Aug. 1909 aged 71; JAMES GREIG d. 14 June 1910 aged 29; above ALEXANDER GREIG d. 22 Sept. 1910 aged 73.

---

27 No Stone

---

28 Erected by her son & dau. G. & R. PAGE in memory of HELEN FORBES PAGE wife of ALEXANDER HUTTON d. 30 Jan. 1908 aged 57; their dau. ISABELLA wife of JOHN FOX-CROFT d. 26 Apr. 1912 aged 42.

---

29 No Stone

---

30 Erected by HELEN GEORGE in memory of her husband JOHN BUCHAN d. 4 Oct. 1893 aged 73; above HELEN GEORGE d. 25 July 1906 aged 88.

---

31 Erected by KENNETH McGREGOR M.C., in memory of his son KENNETH McGREGOR d. 24 Aug. 1868 aged 2 weeks.

---

32 Erected by WILLIAM HENDERSON seaman, in memory of his wife ANN ALEXANDER d. 11 Jan. 1855 aged 47; his mother ISABELLA WILLOX d. 5 Feb. 1849 aged 72; the said WILLIAM HENDERSON d. at Matamzies, West Indies 2 Apr. 1864 aged 54; Also to the memory of THOMAS HENDERSON blacksmith b. 13 May 1814 - d. 10 June 1893 aged 69; his wifeMARY GRANT d. 15 Mar. 1896 aged 86.

---

33 In loving memory of Mother 1908.

J. GORDON aged 39. 1889.

---

34 (Small stone wedged between two) In memory of LESLIE MATHIESON d. 28 June 1938 aged 42.
Erected by ELSIE ADAM in memory of her husband JAMES ADAM d. 15 May 1868 aged 30; their dau. JEANNIE ANN d. 24 June 1876 aged 8.

---

35 In loving memory of JOHN GRANT Mariner d. Apr. 1896 aged 82; HELEN HENDERSON his wife d. Mar. 1885 aged 76; their sons JOHN GRANT Jnr. shipmaster d. Singapore F.M.S. May 1897 aged 53; JAMES H. GRANT boilermaker d. Sydney, New South Wales Aug. 1910 aged 58; ALEXANDER H. GRANT engineer d. at sea near Singapore Dec. 1894 aged 33; also ANN FRASER wife of JOHN GRANT Jnr. d. July 1916 aged 72.

---

36 To the mother of JAMES MACKIE Craiglug, Forglen and of his wife HELEN S. HECTOR. also their daughter HELEN.

---

37 GEORGE GLASS d. Aug. 1917.

Section C.

1a No Stone.

1 Erected by ISABELLA HENDERSON in memory of her husband JOHN STUART d. 6 May 1882 aged 34; their family JOHN d. 14 Nov. 1879 aged 1 yr 9 mths; WILLIAM d. 31 Mar. 1891 aged 21; above ISABELLA HENDERSON d. 2. Feb. 1904 aged 56; dau. ISABELLA d. 26 July 1955 aged 74.

2 Erected to the memory of WILLIAM MEARNS d. 6 Apr. 1936 aged 74; his wife MARGARET LOBBAN d. 26 Oct. 1946 aged 89; their son 2nd Lieut. HARRY GAULD MEARNS d. of wounds 20 Aug. 1916 aged 21.

3 In loving memory of JAMES BISSETT blacksmith d. 14 Oct. 1878 aged 68; their son JAMES d. 24 Aug. 1848 aged 7; dau. ANN d. 1 May 1850 aged 11; son GEORGE d. 27 Jan. 1903 aged 52; WILLIAMINA McKAY wife of above GEORGE BISSETT d. 14 July 1927 aged 77.

4 Erected by MARY WATT in memory of her husband GEORGE ROBERTSON blacksmith d. 6 Nov. 1881 aged 59.

5 No Stone.

6 Erected by WILLIAM HAY millwright, in loving memory of his wife JANE MORRISON d. 18 Aug. 1886 aged 45; their family - ANN d. 31 Jan. 1871 aged 3; WILLIAM d. 24 Mar. 1874 aged 10; JOHN d. July 1875 aged 3; JANE ANN d. 1 Sept. 1882 aged 5; above WILLIAM HAY d. 24 Feb. 1895 aged 62.

7 Erected by CHRISTINA SMITH in loving memory of her mother JANE SIMPSON d. 13 July 1867 aged 87; her father GEORGE BRECHIN d. 12 Mar. 1875 aged 76; their adopted son GEORGE McBAIN McALISTER d. 7 Feb. 1857 aged 6. (Wooden Memorial)

8 (Er)ected . . . . a friend (in me)mory of ROBERT . . . (depa)rted this life 29 Mar. . . .aged 72; . . . of his spouse ISABELLA TOUGH d. 20 Oct. 1843 aged 73.

9 No Stone.

10 No Stone

11 Erected by WILLIAM MELVIN seaman, in memory of his father WILLIAM MELVIN weaver in Aberdeen d. 25 Nov. 1838 aged 79; said WILLIAM MELVIN d. at sea 9 Dec. 1847 aged 50; also JANET DAWSON wife of WILLIAM MELVIN weaver d. 30 July 1848 aged 81; also MARGARET MELVIN wife of HENRY BRECHIN d. 7 Sept. 1899 aged 89.

12 Little BOBBIE

C 13 In memory of WILLIAM LAWRIE seaman d. 29 June 1914 aged 68; his wife JESSIE BIRSE d. 22 Nov. 1892 aged 45.

---

14 In loving memory of my dear husband and our father ALEXANDER GIBSON LAWRIE d. 16 Apr. 1941 aged 61, from his wife and family.

---

15 Erected by JOSEPH MATHER in loving memory of his son JAMES McLEAN MATHER accidentally killed 13 Feb. 1885 aged 18; his nephew ALEXANDER McLEAN accidentally drowned 10 June 1871 aged 18; above JOSEPH MATHER d. 19 Sept. 1926 aged 86; his wife ISABELLA GRANT d. 15 Sept. 1916 aged 78; dau. ISABELLA MATHER d. 1 Sept. 1945 aged 77; JAMES McLEAN d. 3 Feb. 1902 aged 78; his wife JESSIE GRANT d. 6 Apr. 1912 aged 84.

---

16 Erected by JAMES ALLATHAN in memory of his mother MARGARET McGRUER d. 9 Oct. 1851 aged 36; his father GEORGE ALLATHAN d. 12 Aug. 1865 aged 50; ELIZABETH ALLATHAN d. 25 June 1917 aged 66; the above JAMES ALLATHAN d. 20 Jan. 1919 aged 75; his wife JANET MARTIN d. 7 Apr. 1926 aged 80.

---

17 3310 Corporal L. ANDERSON Guards Machine Gun Regt., 14 Aug. 1919 aged 23.

---

18 "FINNIE" and NEAVE.

---

19 Erected by ALEXANDER DUNCAN shipmaster in memory of his father JOHN G. DUNCAN d. 7 Sept. 1867 aged 57; his mother JANET GARROW d. 5 Apr. 1885; In memory of ELIZABETH MATTHEW wife of WILLIAM DUNCAN d. Bellvue, 256 Holburn St., 17 Aug. 1908 aged 64; also his sisters and brothers - MARGARET drowned by the loss of the S.S.Stanley 24 Nov. 1864 aged 18; GEORGE d. 23 July 1867 aged 17; JOHN d. 30 July 1868 aged 24; ANN d. 25 Aug. 1870 aged 18.

---

20 Erected by WILLIAM DUNCAN in loving memory of his dau. MAGGIE DUNCAN (PEGGIE) d. 26 June 1913 aged 9½; his son WILLIAM C. DUNCAN,R.I.C., accidentally killed Duncarvan, Co. Waterford, Ireland 17 Apr. 1921 aged 20½; his father WILLIAM DUNCAN d. 4 Dec. 1924 aged 81; son-in-law JOSEPH ANGUS d. 11 Aug. 1927 aged 33; his beloved wife MARGARET ANN WALKER d. Needham, Mass. U.S.A. 10 Mar. 1952 aged 79; the first named WILLIAM DUNCAN d. Needham, Mass. U.S.A. 17 Sept. 1962 aged 88

---

21 The family resting place of JOHN & ELIZABETH REID CRICHTON. Erected by their son D.W. CRICHTON of Assam.

---

22 Erected by DONALDSON ROSS in memory of his beloved wife BARBARA AIKEN d. 4 Aug. 1881 aged 39; and 9 of his children - 8 boys & 1 girl all died in youth; the above DONALDSON ROSS d. 1 Mar. 1893 aged 57.

C 23 Erected by ROBERT BROWN in memory of his parents ELIZABETH BROWN d. 29 July 1863 aged 53; DUNCAN BROWN gardener d. 29 July 1875 aged 75.

---

24 Erected by the desire of CHARLES GALL sometime farmer in Dally Phoor by Ballater now residing in South Australia in memory of his dau. ELIZABETH d. 18 Aug. 1848 at 24 Gerrard St., aged 10.

---

25 Erected by A.G. McKENZIE shipmaster in memory of his father WILLIAM McKENZIE d. 10 Mar. 1840 aged 36; his mother ISABELLA GOLDIE d. 16 Feb. 1877 aged 67; also HENRY J. FORBES d. 16 May 1868 aged 20 mths; P. FORBES sawmaker, father of the above d. 25 Dec. 1884 aged 54.

26,26a,27,27a No Stone

---

28 In loving memory of my father WILLIAM MUNRO d. 3 Oct. 1918 and of my mother ELIZABETH McDONALD d. 16 Oct. 1918.

---

29 In memory of JEAN GORDON dau. of THOMAS GORDON d. Mar. 1841 aged 8; also JAMES HENDERSON d. 8 Jan. 1870 aged 70; ELIZABETH STRACHAN wife of THOMAS GORDON d. 29 May 1853 aged 41; the said THOMAS GORDON d. 24 Oct. 1854 aged 46; also ANN dau. of said WILLIAM GORDON d. 26 Mar. 1887 aged 85,

---

30 In memory of WILLIAM GEORGE contractor d. 21 Dec. 1887 aged 52; MARGARET SUTHERLAND his wife d. 27 Oct. 1912 aged 66; their son CHARLES NAPIER GEORGE d. 11 Nov. 1919 aged 45; erected by his widow and family.

---

31 Erected by MARTHA FERGUSON in memory of her husband JAMES DUNCAN mason d. 11 Feb. 1841 aged 35; ROBERT their son d. 18 Sept. 1840 aged 4....
(rest of stone embedded in earth - surface very fragile)

---

32 Erected by WILLIAM NOBLE mason Aberdeen d. 17 Jan. 1849 aged 66; his grandson JAMES NOBLE d. 9 Sept. 1890 aged 45; his son GEORGE M. NOBLE d. 11 Oct. 1886 aged 3 yrs 10 mths; ELSPIT MURRAY wife of the said JAMES NOBLE d. 29 Oct. 1902 aged 57; his grandchild ISABELLA T. NOBLE d. in infancy; dau.-in-law ISABELLA TAYLOR d. 28 Dec. 1939 aged 51.

---

33 In memory of GRACE M. MITCHELL d. 14 June aged 16 mths.

---

34 In loving memory of our dear son FRANCIS ROBERTSON 'FRANKIE' d. 22 Sept. 1925 aged 5 yrs 8 mths; his grandfather JAMES B. MITCHELL butcher, d. 11 June 1928 aged 62; his wife MARY MATHIESON d. 2 Feb. 1931 aged 65.

---

35 Erected by ISABELLA DONALD in memory of her father JAMES DONALD d. 20 Mar. 1884 aged 61; her mother ISABELLA CALDER d. 30 Aug. 1893 aged 69; above ISABELLA DONALD d. 21 Sept. 1927 aged 77.

C 36 Surface illegible.

---

37 In memory of MARGARET THIRD a native of the parish of Rathen and wife of WILLIAM ANDERSON d. 23 Apr. 1893 aged 70; WILLIAM ANDERSON a native of the parish of Lonmay and a descendant of the ANDERSONS of East Cairness d. 3 June 1911 aged 85.

---

38 Erected by G.& G. RAMSAY in memory of their mothers MOLLEY TULLOCH d. 5 Jan. 1881 aged 82; CHRISTINA ROBERTSON d. 17 June 1893 aged 85.

---

39 Erected by WILLIAM CAMERON in memory of his beloved wife MARGARET MILNE d. 15 June 1883 aged 49; their son ALEXANDER d. 2 May 1873 aged 1½; son . . . . d. 21 June 18..; the above . . . d. 14 D(ec). . . . also their . . . .d. 16. . . also GRACE beloved wife of JAMES WALKER d. 11 Mar. 1919 aged 58; ANN d. 28 Sept. 1928 aged 62; inserted by MARY CAMERON in loving memory of her dear sisters.

---

40 Erected by PETER MILNE in memory of his son JAMES MILNE d. 22 Dec. 1863 aged 8; above PETER MILNE d. 20 July 1895 aged 76; his dau. ANNIE d. 22 Aug. 1912 aged 46, (wife of JAMES WEBSTER); ANN SKINNER wife of above PETER MILNE d. 13 Apr. 1915 aged 84; above JAMES WEBSTER d. 19 Apr. 1945 aged 82.

---

41 Erected by ALEXANDER CALDER in memory of his wife MARGARET MILNE d. 22 Jan. 1881 aged 66; also of their children WILLIAMINA d. 28 Dec. 1854 aged 2 mths; WILLIAM d. 27 May 1863 aged 3; JAMES d. 14 Mar. 1869 aged 19; ANNIE d. 25 Oct. 1873 aged 21; above ALEXANDER CALDER d. Dyce 3 Aug. 1885 aged 70.

---

42 No Stone

---

43 No Stone

---

44 JANE OGILVIE (Surface practically illegible)

45, 46 & 47. No Stone.

---

48 In memory of ISABELLA PRATT b. 10 Mar. 1827 - d. 28 Oct. 1902; her father and mother JOHN PRATT b. 24 Mar. 1793 - d. 24 July 1837; HELEN DUNCAN b. 8 Mar. 1797 d. 27 Mar. 1885; also ANN DUNCAN sister of the above b. 4 Dec. 1795 - d. 21 Sept. 1881.

In remembrance of little FREDDY

In memory of JAMES ROBERTSON time-keeper, Broadford Works d. 26 Mar. 1895 aged 62; his wife JESSIE McLENNAN d. 15 Dec. 1914 aged 84.

---

49 In memory of JAMES GLASS d. 17 May 1873 aged 55; his son JAMES WILLIAM; also GEORGE d. 24 Jan. 1876 aged 24; his grandchildren d. in infancy 1881; while MAGGIE, ROBERT, MARY & CHARLES GLASS all d. of Diphtheria in 1890.

C 50 Erected by the family in loving memory of their dear father JAMES INNES d. 29 July 1925 aged 78; their mother ELSPET CALDER d. 14 Jan. 1903 aged 46; their family - WILLIAM d. 12 June 1888 aged 7; ALBERT d. 27 Mar. 1914 aged 17; their grandson THOMAS ESSON d. 1 Oct. 1911 aged 2; JAMES ESSON d. 17 Mar. 1916 aged 5; dau. RACHEL beloved wife of THOMAS ESSON d. 19 July 1932 aged 42.

---

51 ARCHIBALD McSHANE Snr., 1851 - 1918; dau. LAVINIA 1889 - 1895

SECTION D.

1 1853 Erected by GEORGE TAYLOR Colr. Sergt. 91st Regt., in memory of his brother WILLIAM FALCONER d. 23 Apr. 1847 aged 16; also ALEX. GREIG rope-and-sailmaker d. 13 May 1902 aged 78.
(Reverse) Also in memory of CATHERINE FALCONER widow of the said ALEXANDER GREIG d. 28 Aug. 1910 aged 82.
(Small stone) In loving memory of MAY.
(Small stone) In loving memory of my dear husband JOHN H. GOLDIE d. 26 Oct. 1916 aged 43; MARY SMITH GREIG beloved wife of above d. 27 Mar. 1940 aged 63.

---

2 Erected by MARGARET PATERSON in memory of her husband KENNETH MacDONALD d. 23 Apr. 1901 aged 71; their sons JOHN & KENNETH d. in infancy; their dau. CATHERINE d. 24 Oct. 1889 aged 24; his sister CATHERINE MacDONALD d. 16 Jan. 1896 aged 68; the said MARGARET PATERSON MacDONALD d. 28 Jan. 1923 aged 84.
(Small stone) J. & K. McDONALD.

---

3 Erected by ISABELLA HARPER in memory of her husband DUNCAN McTAVISH d. 30 Apr. 1884 aged 61; also six of their children are interred here; the above ISABELLA HARPER d. 15 July 1908 age 86; also LAMBERT eldest son of the above d. 31 Dec. 1909 aged 62; ISABELLA MILNE wife of DUNCAN McTAVISH Jnr., d. 8 June 1933 aged 76; their son GORDON d. in infancy; above DUNCAN McTAVISH Jnr., d. 7 Jan. 1944 aged 89 years.

---

4 In memory of our mother JANE ANNE GRANT d. 1879; also eight brothers & sisters.

---

5 In memory of ISABELLA LEITH HAY d. 28 Feb. 1895 aged 1 yr 2 mths.

---

6 In loving memory of MOLLIE THOM aged 17½; DAVID aged 1; INA aged 16; MARY THOM aged 60 years.

---

7 Erected by LILLY in memory of her dear mother MARGARET CALDER CAMERON d. 12 Jan 1917; her father FRANCIS CAMERON d. 14 Apr. 1894; her sister MARGARET CAMERON d. 22 Oct. 1891; her brother CHARLES CAMERON accidentally drowned in South America 14 Oct. 1905; her brother EDWARD F. CAMERON d. 28 Mar. 1929; above LILLY CAMERON d. 12 Jan. 1933; her brother HENRY CAMERON d. 8 Nov. 1934.

D 8 No Stone.

---

9 Erected by WILLIAM B. BRUCE mason, Aberdeen in memory of his son JAMES d. 1 Feb. 1841 aged 2; his dau. ANN d. 1 Dec. 1841 aged 18 mths; JOHANNA d. 25 Nov. 1845 aged 3; JOHN CLARK father-in-law of the above d. 8 Dec. 1845 aged 76; also WILLIAM d. 25 June 1846 aged 10; JOHN d. 30 Sept. 1846 aged 12; GRACE ROSS BRUCE d. 27 Apr. 1854 aged 1 yr 9 mths; also to the memory of JAMES EDWARDS d. 2(-) Feb. 1869 aged 7(0); his wife MARY YOUNGSON d. 3 Jan. 1873 aged 75; MARJORY EDWARDS d. 26 Oct. 1894; ISABELLA EDWARDS d. 9 June 1900 aged 68; ANN EDWARDS d. 24 Sept. 1901 aged 79.

---

10 Erected by GEORGE ANDERSON in affectionate memory of his beloved wife ANN STRATTON d. 18 July 1865 aged 46; her father JOHN STRATTON aged 65; her mother ANN TAYLOR aged 53.

---

11 No Stone

---

12 No Stone

---

13 Erected by JESSIE ROTHNIE in loving memory of her husband WILLIAM CHALMERS d. 24 May 1894 aged 66; dau. MARY CHALMERS d. 19 June 1892 aged 27; above JESSIE ROTHNIE d. 19 Apr. 1933 aged 95.

---

14 Erected by ELIZABETH MOIR in loving memory of her husband JOHN SMITH game-dealer Aberdeen d. 29 June 1891 aged 47; also two children d. in infancy; above ELIZABETH MOIR d. 10 May 1934 aged 86.

---

15 Interred here by ALEXANDER GRAY, Baker RACHEL WALKER his wife d. Aberdeen 28 June 1856 aged 43; ROBERT GRAY their son d. 26 Sept. 1856 aged 3 mths; his son ALEXANDER SPENCE GRAY d. 16 Apr. 1864 aged 3 yrs 4 mths; ROBERT BLAIR, nephew of ALEXANDER GRAY d. 21 Dec. 1878 aged 24; above ALEXANDER GRAY d. 20 Dec. 1881 aged 67; also ELIZABETH BLAIR d. 2 Dec. 1897 aged 78.

---

16 No Stone

---

17 No Stone

---

18 Erected by JAMES BURNETT in memory of MARY, JOHN & ELSIE d. in infancy.

19, 20, 21 No Stone.

---

22 In memory of WILLIE MAIR 1895.

---

23 In loving memory of my dear husband JAMES MAIR d. 29 Jan. 1944 aged 84.

CHARLES McWILLIAM d. 1910.

D 24 1851. Erected by ALEXANDER MacKENZIE painter Stonehaven in memory of his children JAMES d. 9 Sept. 1846 aged 4 mths; ISABELLA d. 29 Sept. 1851 aged 19 mths; above ALEXANDER MacKENZIE d. 30 Sept. 1880 aged 61; MARGARET HENDERSON his wife d. 18 Oct. 1892 aged 70.
(Small Stone) Little JOHN aged 7 mths.

---

25 The family burial place of ALEX. DOUGLAS d. 24 May 1858.

25a Erected by ISABELLA LOW in loving memory of her husband JOHN GLENNIE DAVIDSON Chief Armourer, H.M.S. Canada d. 24 June 1918 aged 38; the above ISABELLA LOW d. 10 Jan. 1935 aged 55.

---

26 Erected by JOHN SHAW in memory of his mother MARY SCORGIE d. 3 June 1885 aged 65; his father DANIEL SHAW d. 4 Oct. 1887 aged 67; also two of their family - DANIEL & JANE d. in infancy; their granddau. JESSIE STEPHEN d. 15 Apr. 1902 aged 27; above JOHN SHAW shoemaker, d. 26 Dec. 1915 aged 63.

27, 28, 29. No Stone.

---

30 Erected in memory of GEORGE ANDERSON gardener d. 9 Apr. 188(6) aged 52; their son GEORGE d. 28 Nov. 1897 aged 15.

---

31 Erected by the DESSWOOD Family in loving memory of Mrs SMITH for 32 years their devoted nurse d. 9 June 1890 aged 72.

---

32 In loving memory of our parents PETER SCULLION d. 25 Dec. 1934 aged 72; ISABELLA COURAGE d. 10 Feb. 1942 aged 78.

---

33 Erected by her husband A. CLUNES in memory of his beloved wife AGNES GORDON d. 20 Feb. 1914 aged 69.

34, 35. No Stone.

---

36 In loving memory of our dear father THOMAS GORDON d. 29 Sept. 1902 aged 62; our mother JANE GOW d. 2 Dec. 1905 aged 66; our sister HELEN d. 9 Apr. 1893 aged 28; also THOMAS, MARJORY & WILLIAMINA d. in infancy; MARY JANE GORDON wife of JAMES DUNCAN d. 30 Oct. 1916 aged 49.

---

37 Erected by JANET McROBB in memory of her husband ROBERT COUTTS d. 13 Nov. 1843 aged 50.

---

38 In memory of THEADORE (sic) MORRISON stonecutter, d. 3 June 1840 aged 59; his spouse AGNES JAFFERY d. 3 Aug. 1868 aged 83; and of their . . . . MORRISON d. 16 Aug. 1848 aged 15.

D 39 Erected by MARGARET & ELIZABETH CRANE in memory of their brothers and sisters who d. in infancy; their brother WILLIAM CONNON d. 4 Oct. 1863 aged 15; their mother ISABELLA SCORGIE d. 6 Sept. 1876 aged 64; their father GEORGE CRANE d. 18 Mar. 1895 aged 84; the above MARGARET OGILVIE CRANE d. 24 June 1910 aged 65.

---

40 Mother's Grave. M.L. 1888.

---

41 No Stone

---

42 Erected by JAMES DOWNIE slater in memory of his wife JANE YOUNG d. 18 Jan. 1864 aged (56?)also his sister-in-law ANN YOUNG d. 20 July 1860 aged 24; also (of his mother) MARGARET BRIDGEFORD d. ..Dec. 1866 aged 80; . . . .ELIZABETH MURRAY d. ..May 1868 aged 57.

---

43 Erected by MARGARET HENDERSON in memory of her beloved husband PETER KENN d. 29 Dec. 1878 aged 63.

---

44 Erected in memory of JAMES SHINIE house carpenter d. 18 May 1867 aged 63; his wife MARY FERGUSON d. 13 Jan. 1880 aged 73; their sons JAMES ROBERT & ALEXANDER SHINIE; also his grandson JAMES SHINIE d. 7 Apr. 1903 aged 39; their eldest dau. MARY SHINIE widow of DAVID ANDERSON d. 11 Oct. 1904 aged 75.

---

45 Small stone - no inscription - urn or vase missing.

---

46 In memory of ISABELLA COURAGE d. 24 Aug. 1877 aged 77; in loving memory of ISABELLA BOOTH wife of ALEXANDER DONALDSON d. 21 Jan. 1912 aged 70; above ALEX. DONALDSON d. 10 Feb. 1919 aged 75; their dau. MARGARET PAUL DONALDSON dearly loved wife of ADAM A. HORNE d. 25 Mar. 1934 aged 55.

47, 48. No Stone.

---

49 In memoriam CHARLES McWILLIAM b. 1856 - d. 1910 also his spouse JANE McWILLIAM KEITH b. 1850 - d. 1940.

---

50 Erected by ROSE ANN DAWSON in loving memory of her husband ROBERT A CLARK baker d. 4 June 1898 aged 42; their dau. MAGGIE ANN B. CLARK d. 27 Jan. 1897 aged 16; son ROBERT killed on H.M.S. Juno aged 22; dau. AGNUS (sic) aged 16½; dau. MINNIE B. aged 14; one son and two daus. d. in infancy; SUSAN ANDERSON mother of the above ROBERT A. CLARK aged 74; also J. BREMNER grandchild of the above d. in inf; also Pte JOHN H. CLARK 1st. K.O.S.B. missing 30 Nov. 1917 aged 21; the above ROSE ANN DAWSON d. 3 Dec. 1923 aged 67.

D 51 Erected by ELIZABETH ALLAN in memory of her husband JOHN TROUP d. Aberdeen 14 Mar. 1851 aged 40; his father ALEXANDER TROUP d. Inverkeithnie & was interred there 5 Oct. 1850 aged 72; his mother CATHERINE MUNRO d. Aberdeen 7 Dec. 1842 aged 55; the said ELIZABETH ALLAN d. 8 May 1877 aged 57; their dau. JANE wife of DOUGLAS McRAE d. 2 May 1888 aged 40; also ELIZABETH TROUP wife of JOHN McMILLAN d. 11 Feb. 1903 aged 35.

---

52 Erected by ALEXANDER HADDEN FRAIN mason in memory of his dau. ANNABELLA FRAIN d. 26 June 1891 aged 8 yrs 11 mths; his brother JAMES FRAIN d. 1 Jan. 1854 aged 1 yr. 1 mth;
(Small stone) In loving mem ory of ANNABELLA FRAIN d. 26 June 1891 aged 8 yrs 11 mths.

---

53 In loving memory of SOPHIA DONALDSON aged 29.

Section E.

E 1a In loving memory of our dear son HECTOR STOTT d. 20 July 1917; our dear Grandma d. 3 Apr. 1918; and our dear son ALBERT d. 29 June 1928.

---

1 Erected by GEORGE BISSET shoemaker Aberdeen in memory of his mother HELEN SKENE d. 26 Sept. 1864 aged 55; his father JOHN BISSET d. 23 Mar. 1865 aged 55; his son JAMES BISSET d. 4 Apr. 1908 aged 65; also MARY BISSET dau. of JAMES BISSET and beloved wife of ALEXANDER SINCLAIR d. 20 Aug. 1909 aged 44.

1/2 Erected by ISABLE (sic) KIDD in memory of her husband JAMES KIDD d. 14 Jan. 1890; also BABY & Wee WILLIE. Also JAMIE and GRANDMA.

---

2 Erected by JOSEPH & WILLIAMINA WALMSLEY in affectionate remembrance of their family CHARLES EDWARD d. 26 June 1874 aged 2 yrs 6 mths; JOSEPH d. 11 Mar. 1879 aged 20 yrs 3 mths; ROBERT JOHN WALMSLEY accidentally drowned at Gravesend 8 Dec 1900 aged 33; and interred there; the above JOSEPH WALMSLEY d. 22 Mar. 1908 aged 68; the above WILLIAMINA WALMSLEY d.19 Mar. 1915 aged 79.

---

3 No Stone.

---

4 Erected by JANE SMITH in loving memory of her husband JOHN FYFE Butcher, d. 4 May 1930 aged 72; his son JOHN d. 17 Aug. 1891 aged 3; the above JANE SMITH d. 7 June 1945 aged 82.

---

5 TAYLOR In loving memory of our dear father and mother.

---

6 Erected to the memory of JOHN HARPER blacksmith d. 4 Jan. 1930 aged 80; his wife ISABELLA MacAULAY d. 8 Apr. 1923 aged 76.

E 7 Erected by GEORGE MITCHELL in loving memory of his dau. MARY S. MITCHELL d. 26 Oct. 1896 aged 10½; also SUSAN d. in infancy; the above GEORGE MITCHELL d. 7 June 1932 aged 70.

---

8 Face Gone.

---

9 Erected by ELSPET PIRIE to the memory of her husband WILLIAM CLUBB d. 9 Feb. 1905 aged 47; also her children d. in infancy;
(Small stone) the said ELSPET PIRIE d. 14 Apr. 1916 aged 56.

---

10 103983 Gunner M. KEENAN Royal Field Artillery 16 Jan. 1919 aged 40.

---

11 The burying ground of GEORGE C. FLORENCE 1906; In loving memory of JEMIMA FLORENCE d. 11 June 1907; the said GEORGE FLORENCE d. 22 Mar. 1912 and his wife BARBARA DOUGLAS d. 25 July 1911.

---

12 In memory of ANDREW W. McINTOSH beloved husband of AGNES HENDERSON d. 26 Dec. 1928 aged 63; their dau. BARBARA JENNIE d. in infancy; the above AGNES HENDERSON d. 25 Feb. 1935 aged 66.

---

13 Erected by ALEXANDER MARR ropemaker Aberdeen in memory of his wife ABIGIAL (sic) LOW d. 30 Dec. 1872; also two sons d. in infancy; his dau. JANE d. 4 Feb. 1877 aged 18; above ALEXANDER MARR d. 9 Jan. 1904 aged 78; son DAVID MARR d. 18 Apr. 1919 aged 52; JANE BRUCE wife of above DAVID MARR d. 18 Sept. 1933 aged 69.

---

14 No Stone.

---

15 Erected by HARRIET COLLINGS in memory of her husband CHARLES MARR d. 28 Feb. 1898 aged 43; their son LEWIS M. MARR d. 9 Feb. 1901 aged 4; above HARRIET COLLINGS d. 2 July 1929 aged 73; their dau. BESSIE MARR d. 12 Oct. 1957 aged 74.

---

16 No Stone.

---

17 Erected by PETER ROBB in loving memory of his wife and children; his son JOHN d. 21 Apr. 1886 aged 1 yr 9 mths; WALTER d. 11 Mar. 1890 aged 3½; JESSIE BARNETT his wife d. 18 May 1906 aged68; above PETER ROBB d. Bridgend Cottage, Craigmillar Midlothian 27 May 1915 aged 80.

---

18 No Stone.

---

19 Erected by SUSAN COUTTS in memory of her husband WILLIAM GUTHRIE d. 23 May 1860 aged ?4; above SUSAN COUTTS d. 18 Nov. 1895 aged 69; also the children of THO(MAS SMITH - JANE & WHIN(+)-N d. in infancy; HELEN NICOL or SMITH wife of THOMAS J SMITH plumber, Aberdeen d. (1)5th Nov. 1909 aged 53; her husband THOMAS J. SMITH d. 8 Jan. 1911 aged 58; her niece MARY ANN H. SMITH d. 13 Feb. 1895 aged 58, relict of late WILLIAM SMITH, Coastguard.

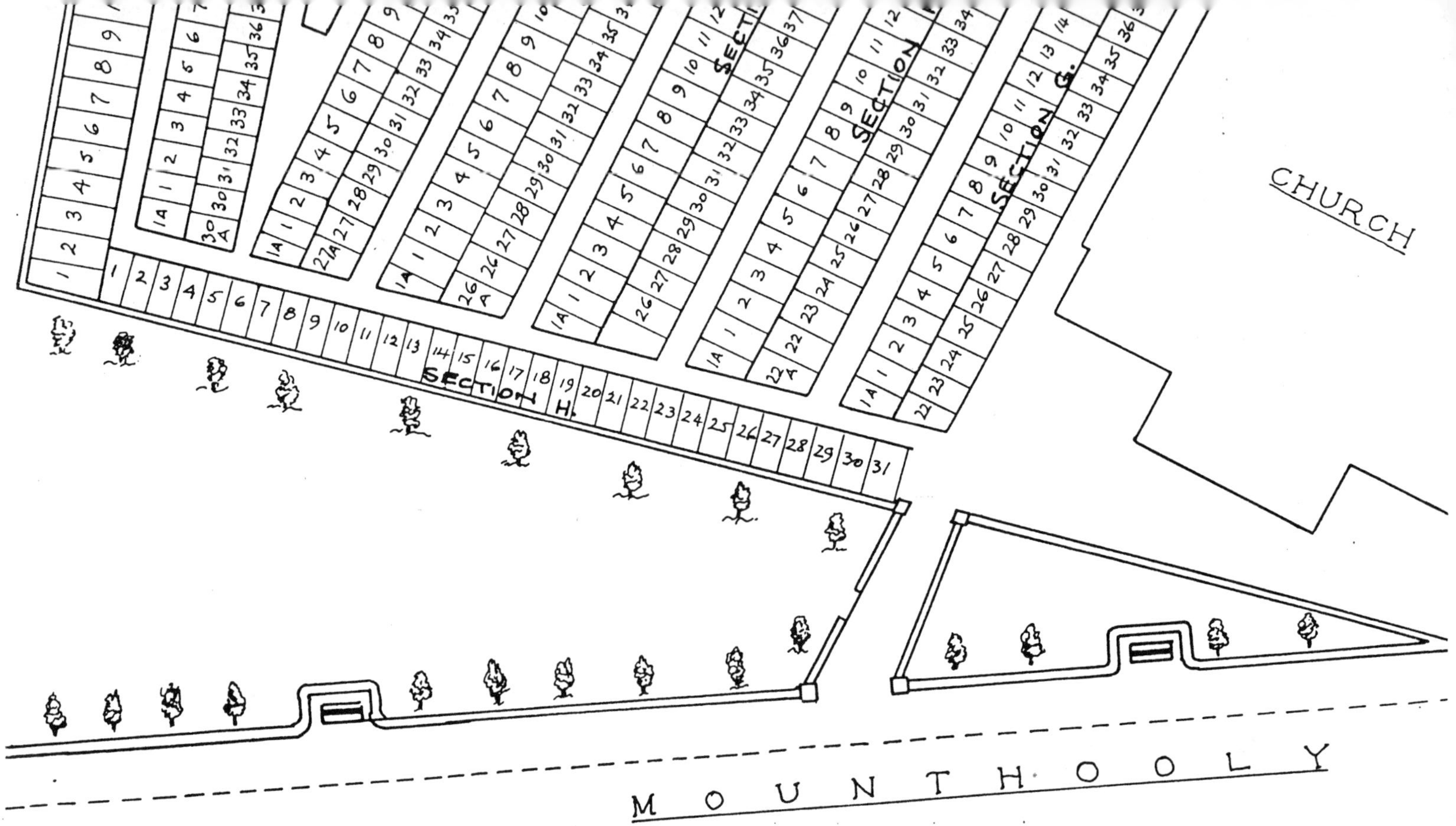
MOUNTHOOLY
CHURCH
SECTION H.
SECTION G.

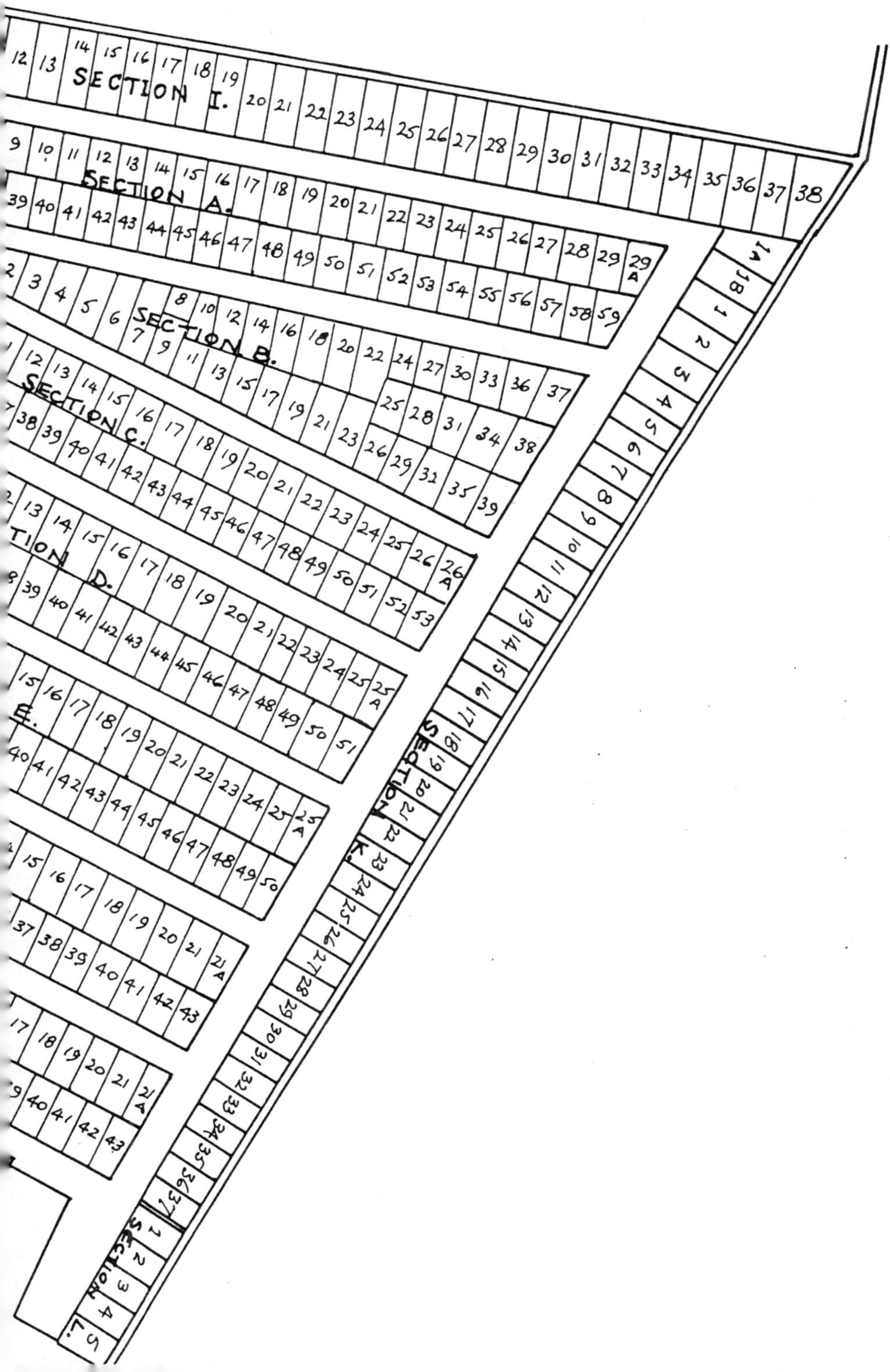
SECTION I.
SECTION A.
SECTION B.
SECTION C.
SECTION D.
E.
SECTION K.
SECTION L.

E19 Contd (Small stone) CRAWFORD E. SMITH d. 3 May 1951.aged 52.

---

20 No Stone.

---

21 Erected by ALEXANDER M. ALLAN in memory of his family HELLEN W.M. d. 14 Jan. 1881 aged 3; MARGARET B.A. d. 29 Dec. 1884 aged 3 yrs 10 mths; ELIZABETH N.L. d. 1 Nov. 1887 aged 7 mths; STANLEY d. 21 Feb. 1895 aged 1; his wife BARBARA ROBERTSON d. 27 Mar. 1914 aged 57; also his gentle HELEN, his beloved wife HELEN MORRISON d. 26 Oct. 1919 aged 42.

---

22 No Stone.

---

23 In memory of ANDREW FOWLER

In memory of W.C. SHAND.

---

24 In memory of little JIM. In loving memory of my only dau. M.J. MILNE d. 12 Sept. 1900 aged 17; my husband WILLIAM COUTTS d. 29 Sept. 1903 aged 64.

---

25 In memory of GEORGE MIDGLEY d. Mar 1875; his wife ELIZA LAWRENCE d. Sept. 1899 his dau. CATHERINE d. Nov. 1919; dau. MARY d. Oct. 1934.

25a In loving memory of DAVID H.B. McLEOD stonemason d. 26 Mar. 1962 aged 53; his wife ANNIE B. CHRISTIE d. 24 Aug. 1962 aged 53; their son DAVID d. 2. Mar. 1933 aged 6 years 6 months. (Small stone) Our Mother.

26,27,28,29. No Stone.

---

30 In loving memory of JOHN GRAHAM d. 8 July 1891 aged 43; his dau. ROSANNA d. 5 Mar. 1884 aged 3; dau. ISABELLA wife of WILLIAM FORRESTER d. 5 Nov. 1907 aged 32 her twin sons JOHN & WILLIAM; his dau. ELIZABETH wife of JOHN SHAND d. 21 July 1908 aged 35.

---

31 No Stone.

---

32 Erected in remembrance of JAMES CROMBIE d. 20 Feb. 1876 and his wife MARY THOM d. 22 Jan. 1870; JAMES CROMBIE eldest son of the above d. 30 May 1889 aged 53; GEORGE their youngest son d. 13 June 1903 aged 51.

---

33 Little BOBBIE $3\frac{1}{2}$.

---

34 Erected by GEORGE WILSON in loving memory of his family WILLIAM d. 3 Sept. 1895 aged 2; BELLA d. 4 Dec. 1900 aged 22; his wife MARGARET CHAPMAN d. 9 July 1929 aged 73; above GEORGE WILSON d. 20 Sept. 1942 aged 89; HELEN d. 24 May 1949 aged 59. (Small Stone) Little WILLIE aged 2. G.W.

E35 In memory of CHRISTINA COULL d. 20 Sept. 1895 aged 2½.

36, 37, No Stone.

38 Erected by CHRISTINA BAIN in memory of DAVID DALGETY weaver, Aberdeen d. 29 Apr. 1890 aged 66; the above CHRISTINA BAIN d. 26 Dec. 1906 aged 75.

39 Erected by ALEXANDER HENDRY in loving memory of his dau. MAGGIE HENDRY d. 13 Mar. 1891 aged 12.

40 No Stone.

41 In loving memory of my dear husband DAVID ALLAN d. 13 Feb. 1902 aged 43; also my 2 sons ALEXANDER killed in action 18 July 1918 aged 38; WILLIAM d. 16 Mar. 1922 a result of wounds aged 39.

42, 43, No Stone.

44 In memory of PETER and GEORGE. Also SUSAN

45 Erected by JOHN MITCHELL in loving memory of his family MARGARET d. 1 Dec. 1888 aged 9½; ARCHIBALD aged 22 mths; MARY aged 22 mths; little MAGGIE aged 7 mths; PETER aged 4 mths; NELLIE aged 12 mths; his mother HELEN GOODBRAND d. 27 Aug. 1893 aged 69; his sister HELEN MITCHELL d. 18 Sept. 1892 aged 39; father-in-law JOHN McINTOSH, poet, d. 28 Sept. 1893 aged 75; ARCHIBALD MITCHELL d. 14 Mar. 1903 aged 49; MARY McINTOSH beloved wife of JOHN MITCHELL d. 14 Dec. 1903 aged 50; ISABELLA McKIE or MITCHELL d. 18 June 1909 aged 56; her dau. ISABELLA d. 13 July 1900 aged 21.

46 In memory of ROBERT MITCHELL aged 49.

47 In loving memory of THOMAS GRAY d. 21 May 1930 aged 76; his wife ANNIE ALLAN d. 8 July aged 66; their son and daus - CHARLES; ANNIE; MARY & BELLA.

48 Little ANDY sleeps here.

49, 50 No Stone.

SECTION F.

1a Erected by WILLIAM BROWN in memory of his wife ELSIE FORBES MARSHALL d. 9 Mar. 1917 aged 67; also WILLIAM BROWN d. 30 Nov. 1918 aged 70.

1, 2, No Stone

F.3 In memory of CHARLES CHATWIN CURRIRE,a native of Birmingham d. 16 May 1881 aged 50; his son ALFRED d. 2 Oct. 1861 aged 4; his dau. ELIZABETH d. 13 Nov. 1879 aged 20, both interred in Inverurie; his son CHARLES d. 15 Sept. 1888 aged 20; his grandson WILLIAM DONALD d. 2 Apr. 1890 aged 11; his dau. MAGGIE d. 10 Oct. 1890 aged 20; son WILLIAM d. 9 Oct. 1895 aged 41; JANE CLARK wife of the above d. 15 Jan. 1912 aged 60; JANE WATSON wife of CHARLES d. 4 July 1918 aged 80 and interred at Edinburgh.

---

4 No Stone.

---

5 H. M.P. BARBARA aged 20 mths; ALICE aged 6 mths; HECTOR aged 8 mths.

---

6 J. H. ANN BROWN HADDEN d. 22 Feb. 1881 aged 10.

---

7 Erected by WILLIAM ALLAN in memory of his wife MARY ANN CATTANACH d. 16 Jan. 1919 aged 56; dau. MARY ANN d. in infancy; son L/Cpl FRANK ALLAN Gordon Highlanders fell in action at Arras 9 Apr. 1917 aged 21 interred in Roclincourt Valley Cemetery; above WILLIAM ALLAN d. 30 Dec. 1938 aged 81.

---

8 Erected by ALEXANDER CUMMING Shoemaker in memory of his mother EUPHEMIA LOGAN d. 13 Apr. 1876 aged 57; his father ALEXANDER CUMMING d. 13 Feb. 1877 aged 66; his son HARRY CUMMING d. 15 May aged 2½; his wife HELEN BOOTH d. 29 Sept. 1884 aged 41; son GEORGE C. CUMMING d. 28 Dec. 1896 aged 22; ALEXANDER CUMMING d. 14 Dec. 1899 aged 58; his son ALFRED Shoemaker d. 16 Dec. 1933 aged 51.
(Small Stone) A.C. our little HARRY d. 15 May 1880.

---

9 Our dear father ALEXANDER GAULD d. 28 Mar. 1882 aged 41; his son W.K. GAULD d. 22 Jan. 1939 aged 56; also ISABELLA KEMP GAULD wife of W.K.Gauld d. 25 June 1968 aged 81.

---

10 Erected by GEORGE COWIE in memory of his wife AGNES COOPER d. 8 Oct. 1876 aged 44

---

11 In memory of JAMES NAIRN d. 6 Jan. 1904 aged 56; his wife MARGARET GAULD d. 3 June 1926 aged 73; dau. JESSIE ANN NAIRN S.R.N., d. 25 July 1953 aged 65.

---

12 JANE M. RIDDLE b. 26 Nov. 1851 - d. 24 Apr. 1878; erected by Hon. Mrs Baillie HAMILTON & Lady HARVEY in grateful remembrance of kind service rendered by JANE M. RIDDLE to their mother Lady ELIZABETH PRINGLE of Langton, Berwickshire during the closing years of her life.

13, 14, 15, No Stone.

---

16 In memory of our father THOMAS MARSHALL d. 10 Oct. 1888 aged 64; mother ANN ANDERSON d. 24 Feb. 1911 aged 93; GEORGE MARSHALL d. S. Africa 1899; BARBARA MARSHALL d. 16 June 1927 aged 76; ALEXANDER MARSHALL youngest son d. 30 Aug.1927 aged 69. (small Stone) In memory of JOHN ROBBIE aged 2.

F17 No Stone.

18 In memory of WILLIAM JOHNSTON blacksmith d. 6 Feb. 1891 aged 63; MARGARET TRAIL his wife d. 3 Jan. 1901 aged 73; son CHARLES d. 2 Dec. 1877 aged 3; dau. ROBINA d. 12 May 1923 aged 60; son JOHN shipwright d. 25 Sept. 1926 aged 61; JAMES JOHNSTON grandson of the above d. Buffalo, U.S.A. 3. Dec. 1924 aged 29. (Small Stone) Little JOHNNY 1884.

19 No Stone.

20 G. PARK 1876.

21 Erected by ISABELLA B. GREIG in memory of her parents JAMES GREIG blacksmith late C.N.S.R. d. 15 Apr. 1910 aged 77; his wife ELIZABETH CRAIGHEAD d. 26 July 1909 aged 68; their family JAMES b. 1861 - d. 1871; WILLIAM b. 1863 - d. 1882; ELIZABETH b. 1866 - d. 1868; CATHERINE b. 1868 - d. 1901; ELIZA JANE b. 1871 - d. 1873; MARY ANN b. 1876 - d. 1893; MARGARET b. 1878 - d. 1880; JESSIE b. 1881- d. 1904; JOHN PORTER b. 1873 - d. 1966; above ISABELLA B. b. 1884 - 1970.

22 Erected by JAMES ALEXANDER in memory of his wife JANE ABLE LEGGAT d. 19 Feb. 1881 aged 64; their children ROBERT aged 3; JANE aged 1; WILLLIAM & GEORGE d. in infancy; aboveJAMES ALEXANDER d. 23 Apr. 1882 aged 72; son-in-law LAWRENCE JAFFRAY d. 24 Feb. 1887 aged 56; SUSAN PETRIE CLEGG granddau. of the above and dau. of A.R. CLEGG d. 13 Nov. 1888 aged 14 mths; MARGARET BLACK ALEXANDER d. 26 Jan. 1909 wife of LAWRENCE JAFFRAY.

22a In memory of JOHN CAMERON d. 25 June 1917 also his wife ISABELLA McINTOSH d. 24 Dec. 1929.

23 No Stone.

24 Erected by FRANCIS JOHNSTON in memory of his wife MARY ROSS d. 17 Dec. 1925 aged 65; also FRANCIS JOHNSTON d. 30 Apr. 1934 aged 76.

25 Erected by GEORGE SIM in memory of his wife AGNES REID d. 1 Jan. 1933 aged 75; also GEORGE SIM d. 10 Sept. 1935 aged 76.

26 MINNIE d. 22 May 1880.

27 (Bottom half of a broken stone) . .also of . . . .ELIZABETH WISLEY d. 14 May 1901 aged 64; the above JOHN PORTER d. 19 June 1920 aged 85; also FRANCIS V. DUGUID d. 26 Apr. 1925 aged 32 husband of AGNES McGUNGLE.

28, 29, No Stone.

F. 30 In memory of GEORGE DUTHIE d. 20 Oct. 1880 . . . . . .(rest illegible)

---

31 Erected by JOHN SMITH in memory of his grandchildren, JOHN SMITH d. 5 July 1879 aged 13 mths; HELEN d. 23 June 1881 aged 13 mths; JAMES C. d. 23 Apr. 1886 aged 13 mths; JANE dau. of the above d. 8 June 1886 aged 25; above JOHN SMITH d. 22 Jan. 1899 aged 69.

32, 33, 34, 35, No Stone.

---

36 Erected by MAGGIE MEARNS in memory of her husband JAMES LAWRIE d. 22 Jan. . . . aged 28; their family GEORGE & ROBERT d. in infancy; her mother ANN STUART d. 1 Aug. 1905 aged 71; her father PAUL MEARNS d. 21 Apr. 1908 aged 81.

---

37 No Stone,

38, 39, 40, 41, No Stone.

---

42 Erected by WILLIAMINA MUIR in memory of her father WILLIAM MUIR d. 30 Jan. 1912 aged 65 years.

---

43 No Stone.

SECTION G.

1a The burial ground of JOHN BAXTER Flesher, Aberdeen d. 13 Jan. 1884 aged 62; GEORGE RAIT painter and ELIZABETH his wife also their dau. ELIZABETH STEPHEN and her son DAVID STEPHEN.

(Small stone) "Mother"

---

1 The burial place of JOHN ANDERSON clerk in Aberdeen. In memory of his mother JEAN HENDRY d. 26 Feb. 1852 aged 55; also JOHN ANDERSON d. 5 Nov. 1886 aged 60.

---

2 No Stone.

---

3 Erected by WILLIAM PATERSON in loving memory of his father WILLIAM PATERSON d. 21 June 1897 aged 66; his mother ISABELLA McPHERSON wife of the above d. 14 Mar. 1898 aged 62.

---

4 Erected by HUGH McPHERSON in memory of his beloved wife ELSPET HENDERSON d. 24 Oct. 1881 aged 59; above HUGH McPHERSON d. 10 Mar. 1886 aged 69; In memory of JEANIE S. WALKER d. 25 Dec. 1895 aged 9 mths.

(Reverse) In memory of ANN LAWSON wife of ANGUS McDONALD aged 62; their son PETER McDONALD aged 26; above ANGUS McDONALD d. 30 Jan. 1908 aged 82.

G.5 Erected by WILLIAM HADDEN in memory of his son FRANCIS T HADDEN d. 14 Apr. 1881 aged 6 yrs 9 mths; dau. EVELYN d. 1 Nov. 1895 aged 7 mths; his wife ANN SUTHERLAND d. 18 Mar. 1921 aged 69; above WILLIAM HADDEN d. 11 July 1936 aged 84.

6, 7, No Stone.

8 (1) ROSE fondest memories of my dear husband BOB.
(2) Wee WILLIE and GORDON ROSE.

9, 10, No Stone.

11, 12 Blank

13 No Stone.

14 Erected by JOHN McLEOD in loving memory of his dau. CATHERINE McLEOD d. 24 Feb. 1883 aged 19; his wife HELEN PHILIP d. 12 Jan. 1890 aged 57; above JOHN McLEOD d. 29 Nov. 1896 aged 66.

15 Erected by EDWARD P. DICKIE Esq., New York in memory of his uncle ADAM DICKIE d. 1 Nov. 1884 aged 74.

16 In memory of GEO. W. LAWRENCE d. 2 Oct. 1884 aged 47; Also MARGARET wife of SIDNEY G HUNT and dau. of above d. 19 July 1900 aged 30; G.W. LAWRENCE grandson of above d. 6 Apr. 1905 aged 1; also AGNES CRUICKSHANK widow of the above d. 12 Feb. 1908 aged 64; dau. JESSIE J. LAWRENCE d. 20 Mar. 1938 aged 63.
(Two small stones) Father's grave; Mother's grave.

17 Erected by WILLIAM YOUNG in loving memory of his wife HELEN KELMAN d. 27 Feb. 1905 aged 56; his family ALEXANDER d. 11 May 1898 aged 29; MARY d. 9 Feb. 1907 aged 24; ELIZA d. 14 Feb. 1896 aged 12; ISA d. 9 Mar. 1900 aged 13; OSWALD d. 29 Mar. 1900 aged 11.

18 Erected by ALEXANDER PATERSON in memory of his brother JOHN PATERSON a native of Banff d. Aberdeen 24 Mar. 1889 aged 86.

19 No Stone.

20 In loving memory of WILLIAM LOW d. 21 Oct. 1898 aged 2 yrs 9 mths.

21 WILLIAM PATERSON MACKIE d. 16 Feb 1906; JEAN BAIN MACKIE d. 11 July 1918; WILLIAM MACKIE Jnr., d. 20 Dec. 1909; JOHN BAIN MACKIE d. 3 Jan. 1916; JOHN WATSON MACKIE d. 24 Mar. 1897; ANGUS MACKIE Pilot Officer R.C.A.F. Killed in action 27 Feb. 1945.
(Small.stone) JOHN W. MACKIE aged $4\frac{1}{2}$ years.

G.21a Erected by WILLIAM McTAVISH in memory of his dear wife JESSIE JOHNSTON d. 5 Aug. 1938 aged 62; their sons JOSEPH & ALFRED &grandson WILLIAM d. in infancy; their son WILLIAM d. 12 July 1940 aged 27; above WILLIAM McTAVISH d. 13 Aug. 1962 aged 87.
(Small stones) (1) In loving memory of our dearly beloved son WILLIAM McTAVISH MASSON aged 5 mths.
(2) In loving memory of ALFRED McTAVISH aged. 1 yr 7 mths. From the family.

---

22 No Stone.

---

23 Erected by his widow and family in loving memory of their dear father JOHN ROBB d. 31 July 1907 aged 65; ANNIE d. 25 Nov. 1881 aged 7½; HELEN d. 20 May 1900 aged 14; our mother JANE ROBB d. 15 Dec. 1925 aged 75; eldest dau. JESSIE d. 25 Feb. 1933.

---

24 Sacred to the memory of ELSPET MILNE d. 10 Jan. 1937 aged 79; her beloved husband ALEXANDER LOW d. 21 Feb. 1937 aged 77; Erected by the family.

---

25 In memory of JANET MURRAY wife of JOHN HOGARTH d. 12 July 1880 aged 58; above JOHN HOGARTH flax dresser d. 4 Mar. 1899 aged 77; his dau-in-law MARY THOMSON d. 3 Oct. 1921 aged 73; her husband PETER HOGARTH d. 21 Aug. 1928 aged 74.

26,27,28,29,30,31. No Stone.

---

32 Erected by ELIZABETH BALFOUR in memory of her husband GEORGE BISSET shoemaker Aberdeen d. 11 Dec. 1884 aged 44; above ELIZABETH BALFOUR d. 1 June 1930 aged 88.

---

33 No Stone.

---

34 Erected by ALEXANDER CAMERON in memory of his dau. MARY ANN d. 29 Oct. 1888 aged 14; his wife MARY ANDERSON d. 16 Sept. 1896 aged 58; above ALEXANDER CAMERON d. 6 June 1903 aged 57; sister-in-law ANN ANDERSON d. 15 Apr. 1905 aged 90; also ALEXANDER CAMERON husband of MARGARET WATSON d. suddenly 24 Feb. 1921 aged 52; above MARGARET WATSON d. 7 Apr. 1927 aged 58.

---

35 In loving memory of HARRY G. SINCLAIR aged 10 years.

---

36 No Stone.

---

37 Erected by ANNIE GIBSON in loving memory of her husband ALEXANDER DAVIDSON d. 6 Sept. 1898 aged 64; above ANNIE GIBSON d. 31 Oct. 1922 aged 79.

---

38 Erected by GEORGE DONALD Spirit Merchant, Aberdeen in loving memory of his parents ALEXANDER DONALD d. 14 June 1897 aged 56; MAY EDWARDS d. 3 Jan. 1901 aged 56; his brother WILLIAM d. 3 May 1909 aged 40; DUNCAN & MADGE d, in infancy.

G.39 Erected by JOHN M. SMITH flesher, in memory of his son SIDNEY d. 19 Jan. 1889 aged 1 yr 4 mths; his sister ISABELLA GORDON SMITH widow of the late JOHN AULD flesher d. 22 Apr. 1891 aged 48; his brother-in-law WILLIAM G. ADAM d. 4 Mar. 1925 aged 76; his/wife RACHEL ADAM d. 24 May. 1929 aged 75; above JOHN M. SMITH d. 23 Mar. 1938 aged 83.

---

40 No Stone.

---

41 In memory of my dear wife aged 52.

---

42. 43. No Stone.

On the wall of the Church:
Rev. HERBERT BELL M.A., for 10 years minister of this parish d. Aberdeen 21 Nov. 1887 aged 45. Interred at Canonbie, Dumfries-shire. Erected by the Congregation.

SECTION H.

1 (Small stones) JOHN & AKKIE Feb. 1880; Little JAMIE sleeps here.

---

2 Erected by GEORGE ANDERSON JNR., engraver, in memory of his mother CATHERINE LESLIE THOM d. 13 Aug. 1910 aged 75; his father GEORGE ANDERSON d. 14 Dec. 1900 aged 68; his sister JESSIE PATTERSON d. 13 Aug. 1883 aged 28; sister MINNIE d. 23 Apr. 1936;also the above GEORGE ANDERSON Jnr., d. 19 Nov. 1944 aged 81.

---

3 No Stone.

---

4 ELIZABETH CRAIG d. Aberdeen 8 Apr. 1848 aged 66. Children of WILLIAM CRAIG her nephew:- ELIZA CRAIG d. 10 July 1866 aged 8; WILLIAM RAMSAY CRAIG d. Jan. 1881 aged 1 yr 8 mths; CATHERINE CRAIG d. 12 Feb. 1890 aged 23; above WILLIAM CRAIG d. Jan. 1893 aged 73; his wife MARGARET GILL d. Jan. 1898 aged 67.

---

5 W. ROBB.

---

6 In loving memory of my dearly beloved son ALFRED (Fred) McKENZIE d. of wounds 16th General Hospital, Rouen, France 19 Oct. 1918 aged 22 & interred Treport Cemetery, France; also GEORGE aged 4; WILLIE & DODS d. in infancy.

---

7 Erected by FLORA McKENZIE in loving memory of her parents KENNETH McKENZIE d. 10 Dec. 1883 aged 57; JANE RAMSAY d. 20 June 1909 aged 74; her brothers ALEXANDER McKENZIE d. 14 Aug. 1905 aged 44; GEORGE C. McKENZIE d. 6 June 1896 aged 26; her sisters JEANNIE; MARY; JESSIE; ANNIE; ELIZABETH & JEMIMA.

H.8 GEORGIE aged 18 months; M.A.CAMERON & BELLA.

9 Erected by GEORGE CURRIE in memory of his father-in-law JAMES BRIDGEFORD d. 20 Mar. 1864 aged 73.

10 No Stone.

11 Erected by . . . ELRICK in memory of his grandchildren ALEXANDER REID d. 18 Dec. 18.. aged 15 mths; also JAMES REID . . . . . .

12 Erected by WILLIAM SUTHERLAND blacksmith in memory of his son WILLIAM d. 6 Apr. 1882 aged 1 yr 9 mths; DAVID d. 5 Oct. 1884 aged 1 yr 7 mths; above WILLIAM SUTHERLAND d. 11 May 1895 aged 51; his wife MARY SHIRRIFFS d. 17 Dec. 1922 aged 68; their son GEORGE FARMER d. 1927 aged 48.

13 Erected by his widow in memory of JAMES JOSS FRASER d. 9 Dec. 1889 aged 58; his father JOHN FRASER d. 28 Feb. 1855 aged 54; his mother JANE CROMBIE d. 6 June 1879 aged 83.

14 Erected by SAMUEL BRUCE in loving memory of his family HELEN ANN & WILLIAM d. in infancy; MAGGIE b. 25 May 1870 - d. 19 Apr. 1893; ISABELLA MITCHELL wife of the above b. 3 Sept. 1842 - d. 21 Mar. 1902; above SAMUEL BRUCE b. 2 Nov. 1842 - d. 30 Mar. 1910; his son SAMUEL BRUCE b. 9 June 1866 - d. 3 June 1910 and interred in Pitsligo Churchyard; his dau. ISABELLA BRUCE ELPHINSTONE d. 21 June 1943; also his grandson FRANCIS M. ELPHINSTONE b. 31 Dec. 1899 - d. 31 Oct. 1941.

15 WILLIAM RITCHIE . . . .; . . . .ADAMS d. 7 Oct. 1887; . . . .RITCHIE d. Mar. 1889; JAMES . . . .: dau. MARGARET ELIZABETH d. 19 Apr. aged 2; . . . . . d. Nov. 1870;

16, 17, 18. No Stone.

19 In loving memory of JOHN HUTCHEON d. 20 Dec. 1950 aged 61.

20 Sacred to the memory of CHARLOTTE ISABELLA EUNSON MAVERS dau. of the late CHARLES MAVERS blacksmith b. 28 May 1858 - d. 7 June 1882.

21 Erected by ANDREW WISLEY to mark the burial place of his beloved wife MARY LAWSON d. 26 May 1880 aged 28; his sister-in-law ANNIE LAWSON d. 3 June 1897 aged 42; his son DAVID WISLEY d. 28 Nov. 1903 aged 28.

22 Erected by WILLIAM YOUNGSON in memory of his son JOHN d. aged 14 months; also MARRON A.B. PRENTICE d. aged 11 months; also the dau. of JAMES & JEANNIE PRENTICE.

H 23 In memory of ANN E.W. CRUICKSHANK beloved wife of JOHN YOUNGSON d. 17 Aug. 1886 aged 32; their triplet son JAMES D. WYNESS d. 2 Aug. 1882 aged 6 mths.

24, 25, No Stone.

26 Erected by DAVID STRACHAN in memory of his beloved wife ANN McPHERSON d. 9 Mar 1895 aged 65; above DAVID STRACHAN d. 29 Mar. 1910 aged 80.

27, 28, No Stone.

29 GEORGE GREIG 1884 also ELIZABETH SMITH GREIG aged 18.

30 No Stone.

31 Erected by ISABELLA WALKER in loving memory of her husband WILLIAM THOMSON d. 26 Oct. 1885 aged 60; their son JAMES WALKER d. 5 Dec. 1895 aged 31; dau. JANE d. 6 Feb. 1900 aged 41; above ISABELLA WALKER d. 12 Oct. 1904 aged 73.

SECTION I.

1 Erected by JAMES MAITLAND in memory of his wife ISABELLA SHAW d. 27 Oct. 1874 aged 24; his 2 children d. in infancy; his twin dau. JEANNIE d. in infancy; his son CHARLES d. 8 Mar. 1886 aged 7; At Greensville, Virginia, U.S.A. ROBERT Nov. 1897 aged 21; above JAMES MAITLAND d. 6 June 1908; ANN AGNES wife of the above d. 26 Feb. 1918; At Aberdeen JAMES 8 Jan. 1908; his grandchildren WILLIAM TUCKER aged 6 mths; Pte. D.M. TUCKER aged 19 interred Aire Communal Cemetery, France; ELIZABETH JANE MAITLAND wife of JOHN M. ANDERSON d. 26 Aug. 1932 aged 63.

2 Erected by TIMOTHY SHAW in memory of his family.

3 Erected by WILLIAM ROBERTSON in memory of his son WARREN d. 28 Sept. 1884 aged 4; his father THOMAS ROBERTSON d. 11 Apr. 1891 aged 73; also ELI ANGUS ROBERTSON d. 5 July 1896 aged 10½; above WILLIAM ROBERTSON d. 30 Mar. 1922 aged 79; his wife JEMIMA ANGUS THOMSON d. 1 Aug. 1929 aged 79; WILLIAM S. ROBERTSON d. 26 Feb. 1939 aged 60; NORMAN McF. ROBERTSON lost at sea through enemy action 1 May 1943 aged 52; MARY ANGUS ROBERTSON d. 16 Sept. 1953 aged 80.

4 Little WILLIE's Grave.

5 Wee ALLAN lies here.
STEWART In memory of MARY ANN BAIN beloved wife of CHARLES STEWART carpetweaver Old Aberdeen d. 6 May 1874 aged 32;above CHARLES STEWART d. 7 May 1898 aged 57.

6 Erected by WILLIAM SHERRIFFS seaman Aberdeen in memory of his wife ANN McKAY d. 12 June 1883 aged 28; his sister ANN DAWSON wife of JAMES BLACKHALL sailmaker d. 30 Mar. 1893 aged 30.

I 7 Erected in memory of JOHN MILNE baker d. 13 Dec. 1885 aged 52; his wife JANE GREIG d. 29 Dec. 1913 aged 83; dau. JANE ALLAN MILNE d. 17 July 1910 aged 54.

---

8 Erected by WILLIAM MITCHELL DRYSDER in memory of his grandmother MARY HOSSACK d. 8 Dec. 1866 aged 84; his wife ISABELLA REID d. 5 Jan. 1874 aged 24; son WILLIAM d. 11 Feb. 1879 aged 5; mother MARY MITCHELL d. 1 May 1890 aged 74; above WILLIAM DRYSDER d. 7 Aug. 1912 aged 61.

---

9 In memory of ELIZABETH BOWMAN who taught a school in connection with Greyfriars Parish for upwards of 30 years d. 12 Apr. 1883. Much respected.

---

10 No Stone.

---

11 Erected by PETER ROBB Sacrist, Marischal College in memory of his daus. ANNIE MERSON YEATS d. 22 Mar. 1881 aged 9½ mths; CHRISTIAN KELMAN d. 7 Oct.1885 aged 13½ mths; his mother JEAN ROBERTSON d. 6 May 1882 aged 59; above PETER ROBB d. 2 Aug.1888 aged 40; JEAN ROBERTSON b. 23 May 1874 - d. 24 May aged 80; GEORGINA b. 5 Sept. 1872 - d. 24 Dec. aged 35; his sons JAMES PARK killed in action 12 Aug. 1916 aged 39; JOHN DUNCAN d. Japan 12 Apr. 1925 aged 42; his wife ANNIE MERSON YEATS d. 22 Jan. 1928 aged 76; son WILLIAM ANDREW d. 20 May 1940 aged 54.

---

12 Wee GEORGIE.

---

13 1859. Erected by ALEXANDER McNAIR in memory of his son JOHN drowned at sea and lies in Kamiesoh d. 18 Dec. 1855 aged 16; his dau. ELIZABETH DUTHIE d. 13 Jan.1859 aged 5; above ALEXANDER McNAIR d. 11 May 1883 aged 76; grandson WILLIAM STOPANI McNAIR d. 20 Apr. 1891 aged 19 yrs 6 mths; dau-in-law EUPHEMIA MURRAY d. 9 Dec. 1893 aged 43, beloved wife of WILLIAM McNAIR; said WILLIAM McNAIR d. 17 Dec. 1903 aged 57.

---

14 Erected by ANNIE RAE in memory of her husband WILLIAM GIBB attendant, Marischal College d. 16 Dec. 1886 aged 53; her 2nd husband WILLIAM CLARK Inspector of Water-works d. 28 Feb. 1898 aged 64; above ANNIE RAE THOMSON d.29 Sept.1909 aged 62.

---

15 Erected by ARTHUR WILSON in memory of his dau. ELIZABETH d. 28 Dec. 1857 aged 3; ROBERT d. 25 Nov. 1862 aged 2½; MARGARET d. 21 Dec. 1863 aged 2; above ARTHUR WILSON d. 5 July 1890 aged 85; his wife JANE LYON d. 5 May 1900 aged 74; his son-in-law PETER GILLIGAN d. 18 Sept. 1900 aged 44; JANE WILSON widow of the above d. aged 67.

---

16 Erected by ALEXANDER PATERSON of the Ganger Institution, Aberdeen in memory of his dau. MARGARET PATERSON d. 15 Dec. 1856 aged 17; DAVID PATERSON d. 8 May 1857 aged 8; above ALEXANDER PATERSON d. 9 Aug. 1874 aged 64; JANE DUNCAN his wife /...

I.16 Cont. wife d. 2 Apr. 1877 aged 62; also MARY ANN MITCHELL d. 14 Apr. 1885 aged . .; STEPHEN PATERSON d. 9 Feb. 1917 aged 41; JANE PATERSON MITCHELL dau. of above ALEXANDER PATERSON d. 9 Feb. 1921 aged 76.

17, 18, No Stone.

---

19 Erected by ROBERT STEWART slater in Aberdeen in memory of his 4 children, HELLEN, WILLIAM, JOHN & HELLEN d. in infancy; his wife ISABELLA RAE d. 26 Sept. 1874 aged 46; his grandsons ROBERT d. 11 Mar. 1877 aged 3 mths; JAMES d. 18 June 1878 aged 2 months; granddau. ISABELLA RAE STEWART d. 12 Dec. 1879 aged 2 mths; son HENRY d. 5 May 1879 aged 2 mths; dau. MARTHA HALL STEWART d. 23 Sept. 1894 aged 53; dau. MARY wife of D.S. DUNNET d. 2 Apr. 1896 aged 29.

---

20 Erected by THOMAS SANGSTER Hairdresser in memory of his mother MARY OGILVIE d. 12 June 1878 aged 56; said THOMAS SANGSTER d. 29 Mar. 1910 aged 63; son ALFRED d. Kansas City U.S.A. aged 27; HELEN McINTYRE wife of above THOMAS SANGSTER d. 4 Apr. 1929 aged 81.

---

21 No Stone.

---

22 In loving memory of ALEXANDER PARK d. 18 Sept. 1883 aged 13 yrs 10 mths.

---

23 In memory of JAMES KEITH d. 21 Dec. 1860 aged 55; his wife SARAH MORRICE d. 28 Nov. 1870 aged 73; JOHN WEBSTER police sergeant, d. 29 June 1866 aged 40; his wife ELIZABETH KEITH d. 7 Jan. 1913 aged 83.

---

24 Erected by MAXWELL IRVINE in memory of his sons DAVID d. 20 Oct. 1883 aged 17; JOHN d. 17 Jan. 1889 aged 6; MAXWELL d. 23 Nov. 1894 aged 16; his wife ANN SIMPSON d. 15 July 1909 aged 64; above MAXWELL IRVINE d. Cleveland, Ohio, U.S.A. 19 Jan. 1911 aged 73; also RACHEL wife of JAMES d. Cleveland, Ohio, U.S.A 21 May 1920 aged 40.

In loving remembrance of D. IRVINE d. 20 Oct. 1883 aged 17.

---

25 In memory of ARCHABLE (sic) PYPER d. 4 Jan. 1869 aged 46; his wife ELIZABETH THOMSON d. 27 Apr. 1884 aged 58; JAMES ANDERSON d. by enemy action Hall Russell 12 July 1940.

---

26 No Stone.

---

27 Erected by ARABELLA B. GIBB in loving memory of her dear husband JOHN MORRISON GIBB granite merchant d. 6 Dec. 1916 aged 42; above ARABELLA B. GIBB d. 6 Jan. 1939 aged 70; elder son ALEXANDER RAE d. Diasagam, Assam 19 Oct. 1946 aged 47 & interred in Shillong Cemetery. their children NESSIE, ALFRED, WILLIAM, BELLA & JIM d. in infancy; JOHN MORRISON GIBB (1901 - 76) his wife FLORENCE MAY HERD (1901 - 81)

I.28 Erected by ALEXANDER GIBB Constable in memory of his family THOMAS d. 15 May 1863 aged 2; ISABELLA d. 20 Aug. 1865 aged 1; JOHN d. 6 Feb. 1874 aged 3; ALICE d. 6 Jan. 1877 aged 1; GRACE B. GIBB d. 16 Apr. 1885 aged 22; above ALEXANDER GIBB d. 16 Feb. 1890 aged 61; ELIZABETH d. 23 Oct. 1887 aged 28; MARGARET d. Leeds 10 Dec. 1891 aged 38; ALEXANDER GIBB Jnr., d. 27 May 1901 aged 47; MARGARET BLAIKIE widow of ALEXANDER GIBB Senr., d. 21 Mar. 1904 aged 71.

---

29 Erected by DAVID TAYLOR in memory of his children MARGARET d. 11 Oct. 1854 aged 1; WILLIAM d. 12 Aug. 1856 aged 5; ALEXANDER d. 7 Aug. 1857 aged 11; DAVID d. 27 Feb. 1859 aged 9; JANE d. 12 Dec. 1871 aged 3; above DAVID TAYLOR d. 15 May 1890 aged 64.

---

30 Erected by JOHN MURRAY in loving memory of his wife HELEN BLACK d. 30 Mar. 1892 aged 40; his children JANE HELEN d. 4 Apr. 1877 aged 8 mths; JAMES ALEXANDER d. Nov. 1887 aged 5; his wife ELIZA BLACK d. 27 Sept. 1925 aged 71; above JOHN MURRAY d. 12 June 1929 aged 79.

---

31 Erected by JOHN GORDON in memory of his children JOHN ALEXANDER d. 8 Dec. 1868 aged 5; ROBERT d. 17 Apr. 1870 aged 5 weeks; GEORGE d. 4 Aug. 1870 aged 2; JAMES d. 24 July 1873 aged 12;
(Small stone under) Little AGGIE'S grave.

32, 33, No Stone

---

34 PETRIE In loving memory of our dear father and mother, also sister and brother DOROTHY & GEORGE also JOHN O'ROURKE, loving husband of DOROTHY.

35, 36, No Stone.

---

37 J. and F. WOOD and father.

---

38 No Stone.

SECTION K.

1a CHRISSIE'S grave.

1b No Stone.

---

1 Erected by ALEXANDER MURRAY in loving memory of his wife BARBARA BLACK d. 7 Mar. 1901 aged 59; his dau. JANE WALKER MURRAY d. 11 July 1899 aged 23.

---

2 No Stone.

K. 3 In memory of JESSIE BRODIE BONNIEMAN beloved wife of JAMES GRAY d. 25 Apr. 1898 aged 39; his two sons WILLIAM & ALEXANDER d. in infancy; above JAMES GRAY b. 13 June 1863 - d. 24 Dec. 1939 aged 76.

---

4 In memory of my dear dau. IRENE JACOBS d. 11 May 1925 aged 4; my father JOHN McGREGOR d. 10 Feb. 1908 aged 55; my brother

---

5, 6, 7, 8, 9, No Stone.

---

10 In memory of WALTER F. SMITH d. 12 Jan. 1899 aged 19 mths.

11, 12, No Stone.

---

13 In loving memory of JAMES & CHARLES KYNOCH.

---

14 In loving memory of my husband d. 22 Mar. 1893 aged 65. W.H.

In memory of JOHN & MARY HUTCHEON and their dau. ELIZABETH d. 21 Apr. 1977.

---

15 In loving memory of our dear MAGGIE.

---

16 No Stone.

---

17 Erected by CHARLES ADAM in loving memory of his son WILLIAM d. 27 Dec. 1892 aged 6; his dau. NELLIE d. 1 Apr. 1897 aged 18; his wife CHRISTINA LYALL d. 7 Nov. 1909 aged 61; the above CHARLES ADAM d. 20 Jan. 1922 aged 75; his dau. ISABELLA LYALL d. 6 May 1940 aged 65.

---

18 Erected by JOHN McLACHLAN in memory of his four children who d. young; his wife HANNAH BEATT d. 20 Dec. 1884 aged 68; above JOHN McLACHLAN d. 26 July 1893 aged 77; dau. HANNAH d. 1 May 1901 aged 63; dau. JEAN d. 12 Mar. 1910 aged 70.

---

19 Erected by ALEXANDER DUNCAN in memory of his father WILLIAM DUNCAN mason, d. 3 Dec. 1878 aged 67; his grandchildren ALICK d. 4 Dec. 1884 aged 13 mths; ALLIE d. 3 June 1890 aged 2 yrs 9 mths; WILLIAM DUNCAN plumber son of the above ALEXANDER DUNCANd. 19 Dec. 1905 aged 25; above ALEXANDER DUNCAN d. 30 Apr. 1921 aged 65; his widow ELIZABETH HUTCHEON d. 16 Sept. 1940 aged 85.

19/20 MAGGIE JANE RAYNER d. 26 Sept. 1892 aged 7.

---

20 (Broken stone) Erected by JOHN MATHIESON in memory of his four children d. in infancy; his mother-in-law MARGARET BRODIE d. 12 Nov. 1864 . . . ; his son GEORGE BRODIE ropemaker . . .

K.21 In memory of JESSIE MATHIESON d. 5 May 1925 aged 82; her husband JOHN K. MATHIESON d. 25 Feb. 1881 aged 44; her husband ROBERT B. MAULDON d. 9 Apr. 1904 aged 57; ROBERT COMBE husband of MARY MATHIESON d. 23 May 1893 aged 44; above MARY MATHIESON d. 6 Feb. 1929 aged 80; ISABELLA C. COMBE dau. of above ROBERT & MARY COMBE (1878 - 1956)

---

22 No Stone.

---

23 Erected by ARTHUR SMITH in memory of his two children HELEN & ARTHUR: his wife JANE MUNRO d. 25 Sept. 1913 aged 52.

---

24 No Stone.

---

25 In affectionate remembrance of ROBERT McB. DUNCAN d. 3 Feb. 1895 aged 18.

---

26 No Stone.

---

27 Erected by CHARLES SIM in memory of his daus. ANNA BELLA SIM d. 30 May 1891 aged 2 yrs 9 mths; MARY M.C. SIM d. 28 May 1909 aged 17; above CHARLES SIM d. 8 July 1925 aged 62; CATHERINE I.E. SIM aged 14 Mths, granddau. of above; ANN E. GIBSON wife of above CHARLES SIM d. 11 Mar. 1938 aged 73.

---

28 Erected by GEORGE PHILLIPS in memory of his mother ELIZABETH PETRIE d. 2 Feb. 1880 aged 79; BENJAMIN PHILLIPS d. 2 Sept. 1886 aged 4; said GEORGE PHILLIPS d. in Germany 12 Nov. 1886 aged 43; JESSIE MAIN widow of the said GEORGE PHILLIPS d. 15 Aug 1937 aged 88.

---

29 Illegible.

---

30 In loving memory of JOHN BLACK d. 4 June 1877 aged 30; his sons GEORGE aged 22 mth JAMES aged 3 yrs 4 mths; ALEXANDER CRUICKSHANK BLACK d. 25 Jan. 1901 aged 28; JOHN FORREST d. 14 Dec. 1935 aged 63.

---

31 No Stone,

---

32 Erected by MARGARET REID in memory of her father JAMES REID shoemaker d. 14 Oct. 1865 aged 54; her aunt HELEN REID d. 7 Dec. 1888 aged 75; her mother MARGARET GRANT d. 12 Feb. 1890 aged 79; said MARGARET REID d. 8 Dec. 1911 aged 65.

---

33 McVOUGH L. JARVIS 1839 - 88; JAMES his son 1876 - 95.

---

34 Erected in loving memory of our dear father ROBERT McFARLANE d. 28 Mar. 1926 aged 87; our mother MARGARET MARR d. 14 Sept. 1926 aged 74; their dau. CATHERINE d. 22 Feb. 1895 aged 13 mths; CHRISTINA WISHART d. 10 May 1957 aged 72; MAGGIE JANE d. 10 Dec. 1961 aged 78; ISABELLA d. 1 Sept. 1967 aged 87.

K.35 Erected by GEORGE MASSON in memory of his mother-in-law d. 1892; his father-in-law d. 1899.

36 Erected by SUSAN CONNON in memory of her dear husband GEORGE MASSON d. 13 Mar. 1939 aged 70; above SUSAN CONNON d. 25 Mar. 1956 aged 87.

37 In loving memory of my dear husband ANDREW MORRISON d. 13 Mar. 1933 aged 61; his son Sergeant ANDREW C. MORRISON R.A., d. 5 Apr. 1942 aged 23; his wife ANN CHRISTIE d. 30 Jan 1965 aged 89.

SECTION L.

1 Rest in peace J.B.

In memory of SALLY WELSH TRAILL d. 3 Oct. 1942 aged 66.

2 1899. Little WILLIE sleeps in Jesus. W.B.

3 In memory of JOHN BEATON hairdresser d. 7 July 1888 aged 78; his wife ELIZABETH LAW d. 21 Apr. 1886 aged 68; MARY ANN SPRINGALL (Pollie) from London beloved wife of W.L. FINNIE Jeweller d. 29 Nov. 1898 aged 46; his 2nd wife BARBARA GRANT or FINNIE d. 9 May 1903 aged 40; WILLIAM LAW FINNIE d. 27 Dec. 1926.

4 Our children MARY GRAY aged 2; ANNIE aged 5; BELLA aged 8.

5 In memory of JAMES SMITH b. 1 June 1827 - d. 9 May 1892.

INDEX